Praise for *Loving My (LGBT) Neighbor*

One of the hardest transitions for the church to make is when something goes from being a warning to a reality. We still talk about homosexuality as if it's something that is coming our way. In this new book, Glenn Stanton provides a clear voice to answer the "what do we do now?" question and to do so in both grace and truth.

JOHN STONESTREET
Fellow, the Chuck Colson Center for Christian Worldview
Host of *The Point*, Breakpoint's daily commentary

Christians and other traditional believers are struggling to figure out how to combine truth and love. Glenn may not have all the right answers, but he definitely is asking the right questions. We will have to learn how to speak about sex, love, and marriage not only with a generic gay person in the room, but as if to a beloved gay child.

MAGGIE GALLAGHER
Author, Senior Fellow at the American Principles Project and co-founder of the National Organization for Marriage

I'm glad to be a friend of Glenn Stanton, despite our many differences, and I'm even gladder he has written a book seeking to make the path to friendship a little easier for all of us. The road is long, but it begins with the spirit of kindness that Glenn's book embodies.

JONATHAN RAUCH
Senior Fellow, Brookings Institute
Author, *Gay Marriage: Why It's Good for Gays, Good for Straights, and Good for America*

I don't know anyone better equipped to write on this issue than Glenn Stanton. He lives it. Glenn is respected around the world, and people from all backgrounds, especially evangelical Christians, look to him for expertise and example on these matters. He is a careful scholar, a brilliant writer, with the keen ability to translate complex matters into pastoral applicability.

RUSSELL D. MOORE
President, Ethics & Religious Liberty Commission
Southern Baptist Convention

There is no cultural issue more difficult to discuss in America today than homosexuality. I cannot think of a single person in America better equipped than Glenn Stanton to engage the questions surrounding building relationships with those we disagree with in a winsome and compassionate manner and helping the church do so.

HUNTER BAKER
Professor of Political Science, Union University
Author, *The End of Secularism*

We have used Glenn's writings to great effect in New Zealand because he has the ability to speak truth but express it in a way that it is difficult to take offense—even when disagreeing with it. This is what he provides his reader in this book: the wisdom, encouragement, and advice in building meaningful friendships with our gay and lesbian neighbors.

BOB MCCOSKRIE
National Director, Family First New Zealand

In the years I debated Glenn about marriage and homosexuality, we developed an interesting friendship. In that friendship there were moments of genuine engagement, for which I was grateful. My hope is this book will open opportunities for others to move beyond the usual talking points and promote real dialogue.

JOHN CORVINO
Chair, Department of Philosophy, Wayne State University
Author, *What's Wrong with Homosexuality?*

How can Christians retain a biblical view of marriage and still engage with friends who are gay? If we are honest with ourselves, it can seem daunting. No condemnation, no kumbaya—this book is a must-read for all Christians trying to navigate a real relationship with LGBT neighbors. Glenn Stanton sheds loving light on how to hold the balance.

ANDREA MROZEK
Executive Director, Institute of Marriage and Family Canada

The issue of homosexuality cannot be dealt with meaningfully without an in-depth understanding of the issues confronting homosexuals. This book shows to us that Glenn has invested time, energy, and resources to do so and as a result, has provided help and advice in this book to the Christian community so that we can discern and learn to separate the person from the politics of the issue.

WEE MIN LEE
President, Focus on the Family Malaysia

There are few advocates for traditional sexual morality among Christians who speak with more civility, understanding, and genuine respect for others than Glenn Stanton. I disagree with him strongly on the basic question of the morality of homosexual conduct. But a lot of people I know would have hated themselves a lot less if they'd grown up in families and communities that actually followed Stanton's example.

DALE CARPENTER
Earl R. Larson Professor of Civil Rights and Civil Liberties
University of Minnesota School of Law
Author, *Flagrant Conduct: The Story of Lawrence v. Texas*

Christians today face a difficult dilemma. How do we remain faithful to the Lord and His Word on the hot-button moral issue of homosexuality while still following His command to love our neighbor as ourselves? Glenn Stanton skillfully balances biblical truth with concern for and friendship with our homosexual neighbors, as he charts a path forward for the church among the LGBT community today. I am so grateful for Glenn's clear, charitable, and God-honoring voice of wisdom at such a time as this!

JANET MEFFERD
Host of the nationally syndicated *Janet Mefferd Radio Show*

LOVING MY (LGBT) NEIGHBOR

BEING FRIENDS IN GRACE & TRUTH

GLENN T. STANTON

MOODY PUBLISHERS

CHICAGO

Scripture quotations are from the Holy Bible, English Standard Version® (ESV®), copyright © 2001 by Crossway, a publishing ministry of Good News Publishers. Used by permission. All rights reserved.

To protect privacy, some names and details of individuals' stories have been changed.

Edited by Elizabeth Cody Newenhuyse
Interior design: Ragont Design
Cover design: Erik M. Peterson

Library of Congress Cataloging-in-Publication Data

Stanton, Glenn T., 1962-
Loving my (LGBT) neighbor : being friends in grace and truth / Glenn T. Stanton.
Includes bibliographical references.
ISBN 978-0-8024-1214-0 (paperback)
1. Homosexuality—Religious aspects—Christianity. 2. Sex role—Religious aspects—Christianity. 3. Love—Religious aspects—Christianity. I. Title.
BR115.H6S73 2014
261.8'35766—dc23
                    2014016938

We hope you enjoy this book from Moody Publishers. Our goal is to provide high-quality, thought-provoking books and products that connect truth to your real needs and challenges. For more information on other books and products written and produced from a biblical perspective, go to www.moodypublishers.com or write to:

Moody Publishers
820 N. LaSalle Boulevard
Chicago, IL 60610

1 3 5 7 9 10 8 6 4 2

Printed in the United States of America

To my handful of friends who labor on the other side
of this issue but are still willing to be my friend anyway.
You know who you are, but you don't know how much
I appreciate who you are, the manner in which you do your work,
and the honorable ways you engage those you disagree with.
My life is richer for knowing you and being able to call you my friend.
Honest.

Laud Him, all peoples!
For His lovingkindness is great toward us,
And the truth of the Lord is everlasting.
Psalm 117 NASB

CONTENTS

FOREWORD

Not long ago, Glenn Stanton invited Jonathan Rauch, a noted author, journalist, and gay rights advocate, to address members of our team at Focus on the Family. Glenn and Jonathan have been friends for some time despite representing opposite ends of the spectrum in the national debate over homosexuality. You can read more about their friendship—and Jonathan's unique visit to Focus headquarters—in the pages of this book.

Something struck me in the days leading up to Mr. Rauch's visit. On the one hand, you had an outspoken gay journalist who had agreed to travel alone to the unfamiliar environs of Focus on the Family and evangelical Christianity. On the other hand, you had some of our team who seemed a bit uncertain how to respond to this man's presence among us.

Now, don't misunderstand me. At Focus on the Family we're 100 percent committed to the biblical view of human sexuality. We believe that sex is given by God as an expression of love to be shared and enjoyed between a husband and a wife. And we believe that the Bible is clear in its teaching on homosexual practice as sinful, as with all sexual activity outside of marriage. Christians cannot change or challenge this as self-appointed editors of the Bible.

So the question wasn't, "What do we believe?" Rather, it was, "How do we honor those beliefs when interacting and engaging with someone who does not share a Christian worldview—who does not accept the Bible as an authority on *any* issue?" It's an important question.

And it's the same question being asked by Christians everywhere as homosexuality and same-sex "marriage" gain acceptance. There's a good chance you already know someone who identifies as gay—perhaps a family member, a friend, or a coworker. Maybe you've found yourself challenged on your biblical beliefs on this subject, even on a regular basis.

The question remains: How do we stay faithful to the teaching of Scripture and yet live in the real world with men and women who identify as lesbian and gay? Why is it that Christianity holds that homosexual practice is not God's will for us, and how do we stand for what we believe in a solid and unwavering commitment to both truth and love? What do you say when a gay coworker invites you to his "wedding"? How do you respond when your daughter asks to bring her lesbian partner home for Thanksgiving dinner? What happens in the business world where values and commerce collide?

These are the types of questions that aren't so easily answered, even when your allegiance to the biblical model of human sexuality is rock solid. But these are the types of questions that you and your children are likely to face in the coming years, if you haven't already.

That's why Glenn's book is both timely and helpful. It reminds us that there are some things on which we can't compromise—namely, the teaching of Scripture and the historical position of the church. But at the same time, there are areas of this debate in which *nuance* is critical to our Christian witness. It's possible that through prayer, wise counsel, personal conviction, and the nature of our relationships with the individuals in question, equally committed believers might take different approaches when it comes to engaging with their LGBT family members, friends, and neighbors. What are those times? Which situations have no room for nuance?

Above all, how do we truly honor Christ as we engage with this issue? As you'll read in the pages ahead, the answer is that we must consistently present Jesus as John describes Him in Scripture, "full of grace and truth" (John 1:14). Grace. Truth. These are the essential principles that will pave the way forward as we interact with homosexual family members, friends, and colleagues, and we must be equally faithful to both. Glenn helps us do this through his insight and years of experience engaging this issue.

JIM DALY
President, Focus on the Family

PREFACE

THE GREAT EQUALIZER

This book is about making and being friends with people who are different than we are.

Everyone, by various measures, is different from everyone else. This book deals with substantial differences around an issue that is taking up a great deal of the oxygen in the room of our public life together. Much of this is uncharted territory, as will be addressed in the coming pages. But it is important to establish that everything you'll read in this book is framed by six fundamental truths that we must keep in mind as we move from page to page, chapter to chapter.

They are not specific to the topic of this book but are essential to it. They are universal truths for every Christian who desires to live under the character and authority of God and His Word. Being universal, they *most certainly* apply to the topic we are exploring here and the people it involves on all sides of the issue. These six truths are:

1. Everybody is a human person. *No exceptions.*
2. Every human person is of inestimable worth and value, none more than another. *No exceptions.*
3. Everyone is deeply and passionately loved by God. *No exceptions.*

4. Unfortunately everyone is burdened with a terminal illness: sin. *No exceptions.*
5. All, as children of Adam, are tragically separated from God, but this does not diminish God's boundless love for us. But it does devastatingly hinder our relationship with Him. *All of us, no exceptions.*
6. Therefore, everyone is in desperate need of repentance, healing, and a new life that comes only in surrender and submission to Christ. *No exceptions.*

This is mere Christianity. These points are the great equalizers of humanity, putting us all in the same boat for good and for bad, proclaiming that no one person is better or worse, loved more or less, nor more or less deserving of love than another. This portion of the prayer of St. Ambrose is fitting when thinking about where all of us stand before God. It is chiefly true about me.

I, a sinner caught by many snares,
seek safe refuge in you.
For you are the fountain of mercy.
I would fear to draw near to you as my judge,
but I seek you out as my Savior.
Amen.

This, or something like it, is the first prayer each of us must give to God on the road to becoming His children, fully embraced by His love.

His love is open to all and our remorse over our sin is required of all, making each of us equal to one another.

INTRODUCTION

IS THIS REALLY WORKING FOR ANYONE?

I live in a unique and interesting world.

I work for a large, conservative, unapologetically Christian organization dedicated to defending the family and helping it thrive. Not only do I buy into what this organization stands for, I am deeply committed to it and its mission. It's what has kept me in, and thoroughly enjoying, this line of work for twenty-plus years, my first job out of the university. But there's another important part of what I do at Focus on the Family that makes my work particularly exciting. While I spend the bulk of my time writing, researching, and teaching on the family as a universal social institution, I also get to hang out, engage, argue, travel, eat, and become friends with those who live on the other side of the same-sex marriage issue from me.

You see, I get to debate this issue many times a year and have done so for more than a decade at universities and colleges all over the country. In doing this I have had the privilege of developing some genuine and mutually trustful relationships with those I engage on the other side of the issue. These people are important to me and truly make my life richer. And I don't cherish these relationships for some superficial "can't-we-all-just-put-our differences-behind-us-and-get-along" symbolism, nor do they with me. We disagree on and debate the important points of our contrasting convictions, but we still admire and esteem one another. Yes, it can happen. And my purpose in this is not just so that I might lead them to Christ, either. No one likes to be someone's project, evangelistic or otherwise. Nor is it so that I might gain more time to argue with them on why this homosexual thing is wrong.

Genuine friendship is an end in itself. Other things might stem from it, but being in relationship only for what it can bring is not friendship.

It's that I truly like each of these friends and *being* their friends, and it shakes up the whole oil-and-water assumption. They are good people, and developing such friendships makes life more interesting. I am always open for more such friendships and will take all I can get.

Many years ago, our family lived in a community with a common pool and hot tub. Some evenings, after we put the kids to bed, I would go over to the hot tub and relax my muscles and tensions from the day. Often the couple living behind us was there as well. I would look forward to joining them and we would sit, soak, and talk about our work, the various issues of the day, the HOA (homeowners association) nazis and their latest craziness. We enjoyed spending time together. They were a middle-aged lesbian couple.

> Since when was it decided that people who see the world in polar opposite ways can't be friends?

In fact, one of them, many years ago, worked where I work. When I would come back home, my wife, Jackie, would sometimes jokingly ask, "Were your girlfriends there?" The first time she asked me that, I told her, "Sister, what happens at the hot tub stays at the hot tub!"

Many might see these two parts of my life as contradictory. I see them as essential. And my bosses and peers at work welcome and enthusiastically encourage me in these relationships because they see the importance of them as well. I am glad they do. Many of my colleagues also pursue and treasure similar relationships, whether with atheists, pro-abortion advocates, or even those strange little folks, the Unitarians. They all see the importance of mixing with people who see the world differently than we do. I believe all Christians should go and do likewise.

I know what you might be thinking, because I get the question quite often: How could I oppose same-sex marriage and civil unions—actively working against them, in fact—and be meaningful friends with those who are involved with and advocate for these practices? Isn't that inconsistent?

The answer is as simple as it is blunt: *not at all.* Since when was it decided that people who see the world in largely polar opposite ways cannot be genuine friends? *In fact, shouldn't we seek meaningful friendships with such people?*[1] Indeed we should, because it helps us understand why those we disagree with believe as they do and what motivates them. It beats operating from stereotypes and lobbing accusations over the wall at each other.

It's no fun living life like it's an evening cable talk show. I like it when others ask hard but honest questions of me, seeking to gain such an understanding of my beliefs. It's actually a sign of respect to bother to really understand what it is that another person believes and why. And it's hard to speak cheaply or ill of those who are your friends.

Hearing from the "Other Side"

I have been hosting a seasonal lecture series for many years at work where I bring in thought leaders who have important things to say about

---

1. In considering developing such relationships—as discussed through these pages—there are a few factors that must be considered by each of us: Are we spiritually and emotionally mature enough to develop such relationships without our faith and values being weakened? Do we struggle with same-sex attraction or other sexual issues where such a relationship would put us in an unhealthy situation? Do you know the parameters you should establish for such a relationship before entering it? These questions should be considered with wisdom and prayer.

the family and its place in the contemporary world. Sometimes these are people who might not agree with us on every issue but whose insights help our team be better students of the family. These events are fun and stimulating, much appreciated by our staff.

One of the more provocative invitees was Jonathan Rauch, a friend who I think is simply the best spokesperson and defender of the case for same-sex marriage around. He is a brilliant thinker, a remarkably gifted writer, and a very nice man who lives in the DC suburbs with his spouse.[2] I have known Jonathan for many years and greatly enjoy our discussions together. As with any relationship, the more we get to know each other, the more comfortable we become and the deeper our conversations go. I wanted to have our folks hear from Jon to experience for themselves what the best case for same-sex marriage sounds like, so that we can work from what our opponents actually believe, rather than what we assume they believe. Very important for any partisan. So, here we had one of the most prominent and persuasive same-sex advocates being invited to Focus on the Family to speak, unscripted and unedited, to a roomful of our employees. One has to be careful with the public dissemination of news like that, right?

"Can you believe that Focus on the Family is now having leading homosexual activists instruct their employees on why same-sex marriage is a good idea? *What is going on over there?*" It's a bit deeper than that.

When I proposed this invitation to our executive leadership, their response was positive because they recognized the value of such an experience for our employees, as well as for Jonathan and the nature of the larger debate itself. And I've been blessed with having earned a bit of trust from our leadership in hosting such guests. I was delighted to get a thumbs-up and so I extended the invitation, and Jonathan very kindly and excitedly accepted. I heard nothing but encouragement and thank-

---

2. It is a struggle to find the right terms when speaking of such relationships, terms that are necessarily descriptive, but also true to our convictions. This is something we must wrestle with.

fulness from employees about what we were doing with this event and how; not because we were "diversifying" but because we were seriously seeking to learn what our opponents actually believe, by . . . actually listening to what they have to say.

So he came. In addition to the ninety minutes set aside for his talk and Q&A, he asked if I would set up a series of meetings throughout the day with our key ministry teams of my choosing. I made sure it was a full day of valuable meetings.

The morning of the lecture, the room was filled to larger capacity than it typically is for such events. Did they come to watch, or to start the fireworks? I wondered. I introduced Jonathan, spoke of our friendship and my genuine esteem for him and his work, and shared a fun story from our relationship. He stepped to the podium and received spirited applause. So far, so good. He gave an excellent talk. But he had been in control of the mic. Now we came to the open Q&A session where employees could ask anything they wanted. Maybe this was where things would get ugly.

They didn't. Each person who stood to ask a question thanked him heartily and sincerely for being willing to come and address us. They noted that it likely was not easy for him. Their questions were honest and pointed but kind: hardballs, thrown gracefully. I was so delighted to hear this. And Jonathan enjoyed it. They weren't dodging the critical points of disagreement or confusion but engaging them in a respectful and passionate way. It was a beautiful demonstration of how engagements like this could and should go. I was proud of my colleagues and of Jonathan.

When we wrapped up the event, the audience gave Jonathan a standing ovation. Not because they were convinced or swayed by what he had to say but as a genuine sign of respect, thanks, and appreciation toward him. We were both surprised. I had not arranged that, nor did I instruct the group beforehand to "Pleeeasse behave yourselves and be nice to the gay man!" It just happened and happened naturally because it was in their hearts to do so. A leading same-sex marriage activist got a standing ovation while in the belly of the beast of the "antigay" movement. *This was not an* Onion *article.*

The rest of the day in the various meetings went just as well. In a few of them, something happened that I have never seen happen in any meeting in my two decades at the ministry. As we got up to leave to our next meeting and the group said their goodbyes to Jonathan, a few asked him—male and female—if he would be comfortable if they hugged him before he left. Wow. And they were unmistakably sincere in this. Jonathan, like all smart people, never refuses a hug and he didn't that day.

Sincere regard and warmth can take place between those who live at extreme ends of such a social chasm. And they should, even when neither compromises on any part of their convictions. That is not needed for civility but mutual respect and kindness in the midst of it is. And that's largely what this book is about. As Christians, how do we live well between the two seemingly polar worlds of...

(1) Our faithfulness in belief and practice to what Scripture and the church has taught from earliest days on sexual ethics, and

(2) Our desire to treat our same-sex-attracted[3] family members, friends, and coworkers with graciousness and acceptance?

---

3. In this book, using descriptors for same-sex-attracted people can pose various problems for many on each side of this issue. I will often use the phrase "same-sex-attracted" because it is a straightforward and factual description, generally free of social, personal, and ideological connotations. But I will also use other terms, not as some way of endorsing or condemning anyone but simply because that seems the best word to use in a certain context. I am also sensitive when sentence structure or clear communication requires the use of terms like "those people" and the like. A superior, finger-pointing posture should not be assumed. As you will see in the next chapter, other words and signifiers that are typically used to refer to same-sex-attracted people can be very imprecise, not really descriptive of everyone who is attracted sexually and romantically to people of their own sex. The topic of what names and words to use and not use, as well as why and why not, is an important topic for those on each side of this debate. Often the answers are not black-and-white.

This balance is very difficult, evidenced by the fact that so many of us struggle so deeply with it, unsure of the proper balance of doing both without compromising on either. It is important we get this right in order to be really faithful to our beautiful Lord and His Spirit.

- Should we love and accept our same-sex-attracted family members and friends or should we put up a wall that clearly delineates our differing moral convictions?
- Can I support "gay rights"?
- What about the couple who wants to be a part of my local church?
- What if they want to accept Christ, but don't see their relationship as sinful?
- I've been invited to a same-sex wedding. Should I go?
- If I vote in favor of laws protecting natural marriage, am I being unfair to my gay and lesbian neighbors?
- Should I apologize for the behaviors and attitudes of other Christians toward the LGBT community?

There are so many questions like this that demand good answers, because they involve both the lives of real people and the integrity of our faith. And we will address them and so many more throughout this book.

Is This Working for Anyone?

How many of us feel good about how we are handling this issue in the church in general? How many of us believe we are doing this well from a careful and intentional Christian understanding? I think we seem to be just fumbling through it, trying to do our best, but largely failing to get much of it right. These are uncharted waters for the contemporary church and we must think well about how we should navigate them given our allegiance to Christ. And then we must *act* well.

> To love God is to honor Him. One primary way to honor Him is to obey what He has taught through His Word.

Unfortunately, it seems like we can only live at one of two extremes: unbending, unfeeling disapproval of all things homosexual or uncritical acceptance of the same. Like many issues, it's not that simple. But we have a faith that doesn't change with the seasons, so how do we live faithfully in light of such issues, and what does that even mean? Again, to some I believe it means only "take a stand and fight" while to others it means "love them and don't make waves." There are other options, and I believe that is where the truth lies.

Our focus in this book will be to seek wisdom, guidance, and most importantly, healthy, real-life examples from solid believers showing how to do this well. As a starting place, faithful Christians must always ask first and foremost what God commands and demands of us. So this is where we will begin.

What Does God Command?

The first question of any Christian must be "What does Christ desire of us?"[4]

---

4. The very popular question "What would Jesus do (WWJD)?" can be problematic. When asking this question of ourselves in a particular situation, we should consider John the Baptist. He was our Lord's cousin and the man whom Jesus declared there was none greater (Luke 7:28). John had a very different calling, personality, and temperament than Jesus. He looked people right in the eye, pointed his finger in their chest, and told them to stop sinning. He had not an ounce of subtlety in him and his primary message was "Repent and be baptized!" Jesus did it a bit differently, often much softer, but not always. We could challenge John's harshness with the question "WWJD?" intimating that John should change his approach, be more like Jesus. But Jesus never corrected John, explaining his tone might run people off. In fact, Jesus came to submit Himself to John's baptism at the start of His ministry, which made John very uncomfortable. We should indeed ask "WWJD?" but not assume that always means speaking softly and with no demands. John didn't always do what Jesus would do the way HE would do it, but he did do what Jesus called him to do.

And how do we know what God wants of us?

God made it quite simple for all of us to know clearly whether we were obeying Him or not. He gave Moses ten straightforward, crisply worded commands to guide all our behavior. Ten! You can memorize them in very little time.

Then Jesus, God made flesh, comes to us and makes it simpler, at least in terms of number. He gives us two. You can write them in the palm of your hand, if not your heart.

The first is clear and unsurprising: *Love God with every part of you and with everything you have.*

The second is clear, but unexpected: *Love your neighbor as yourself.*

Is it safe to say we struggle with doing and understanding number two more than number one? Jesus knew we would, given the gentleman who immediately asked Him, "Who is my neighbor?" Jesus' answer is startling. You can read about in it Luke 10:25–37.

These two commands of our Lord are directly related to our topic here.

To love God is to honor Him. One primary way to honor Him is to obey what He has taught us through His Word. To ignore or rewrite them is to dishonor Him. This is not love.

So what about this "loving our neighbors" thing? What did God say about that?

It can be complicated. Jesus tells us that even (maybe even especially) our surest enemies, the worst of people, are also our neighbor, requiring our love. If they become hostile and get in a good slap of one of our cheeks, we are to make it easy for them to slap the other. If they steal our coats, we are to ask them to take our shirts as well. It's right there in Matthew 5:39–41:

"But if anyone slaps you on the right cheek, turn to him the other also. And if anyone would . . . take your tunic, let him have your cloak as well. And if anyone forces you to go one mile, go with him two miles."

Of all the other things that Christ taught us about living with

> So how do we love our neighbors as ourselves when it's our gay and lesbian neighbors we're talking about?

others, these are among the most basic. He told us so. But we tend to live more by the "eye-for-an-eye," "you-did-this-to-me, so-I'll-do-the-same-to-you" code of neighborliness. It's only fair, right? Well, nothing in Christianity is really *fair*. It knows no such economy, turning fairness absolutely on its head.

So, how do we love God with all our heart, mind, and soul and our neighbors as ourselves when it's our gay and lesbian neighbors we're talking about? Are we exempt from loving *them*? How do we love them? How do we receive them, befriend them, and even disagree with them with graciousness? How do we do all this in a way that pleases our Lord?

These are colossal questions for Christians today, and they cannot be ignored. They matter because they concern people, and that always matters because *all* people are created with a unique part of the image of God in them.

We wrestle with these questions at a unique time. We are confronting something the church has not faced in its two thousand-plus year history. Scary stuff, that. But then, as we see in Scripture, every age has faced its own particular challenges...

We've Not Seen This Day Before

The Bible is clear that each generation must be mindful of the particular age and setting it occupies on the stage of history. Today is not the same as yesterday, nor will tomorrow be the same as today. Each generation lives in a unique age as God's divine and sovereign history moves along. Two Scriptures come to mind in considering these challenges facing each generation.

- In Acts 13, Paul is preaching the gospel of Christ to the Jewish leaders in Antioch and tells them about King David, praising him as one who "served the purpose of God in his own generation" (v. 36).
- In 1 Chronicles 12 we read of those godly warriors who were called to overthrow the evil rule of Saul and place David on that throne as God's servant to the people of Israel. There were many tribes with various tasks in this effort, but most famous was the tribe of Issachar, described as "men who had understanding of the times, to know what Israel ought to do" (v. 32).

Note these words in each verse: "had served" from Acts and "had understanding" from Chronicles. These are the gifts each group was equipped with for their specific jobs. It's what they brought to the table in faithful obedience.

The second set of words is "in his own generation" and "of the times." They speak of *when* these men did these things. Their time and talents were for that unique day, that particular generation and its own challenges and opportunities. At any other time the need and skill set would most likely be different, requiring different kinds of people with different gifts. But *these* folks were for this time.

They had to discover and act on their wisdom and skills for their unique times in the history of God's unfolding story. We must all develop and use the gifts that our unique times require. This is precisely what these texts say to every new generation of the church. Doing this well is what it means for the church to be prophetic in its particular age, faithfully living out and proclaiming God's grace and truth to each age.

To be honest, when I consider that I am part of this generation, facing these unique and important challenges, it scares me. It is like realizing you are now the adult and you can't rely on your parents to bail you out anymore. You're the one in the batter's box. The pitcher is throwing his best heat at *you*! You've been chosen to go to the plate because the manager, for some crazy reason, thinks you have what it takes. You can't ask him to put in someone else. You better have that quiet confidence needed for the task. But sometimes the challenge seems too great, too demanding, too difficult. But here we are, on the field at this moment in time, and the cavalry is not going to come and step in. We are the cavalry! We must have faith in the One who saw fit to put us here according to His great timing.

But why is this time so unique?

The church has never had to ask itself "How do I love my gay neighbor?" in the way we are asking today, because what we're experiencing in our generation is historically unprecedented. This is explained carefully and in great detail in Professor David Greenberg's magisterial history of homosexuality from pre-antiquity to the present, *The Construction of Homosexuality*. He explains that it was not until the 1960s and 1970s, starting in the United States, and then spreading to England and Western Europe, that anyone had either identified or proclaimed himself as "gay." And this was not just because the word itself had never been used, but because it was developed to describe something altogether new in history: a very spirited and energetic social/political movement of identity based on same-sex sexual relations and identity.[5]

Yes, the church has had to deal with the existence of and advocacy for all kinds of sexual relationships from time to time, as clearly explained in both the Old and New Testaments, including homosexuality. But it has never faced anything close to the full-court press exerted by

---

5. David F. Greenberg, *The Construction of Homosexuality* (Chicago: University of Chicago Press, 1988), 458–81. Interestingly, his explanation of the development of this new movement originated because of economic developments in the United States, England, and Europe. "The gay movement arose toward the end of an exceptionally long period of economic prosperity [which allowed and encouraged young adults to seek] self-expression and self-realization, rather than conformity to externally imposed behavioral standards" (pp. 459–60). Of course, this not only contributed to the growth of the "gay liberation" movement but the larger sexual revolution of the 1960s and 1970s itself.

so many influential and powerful voices in politics, media, the arts, and business. These voices seek—no, *demand*—unquestioned acceptance of and full respect for gay, lesbian, bisexual, and transgendered sexual mores and practices, and seem to be more pressuring every month. They insist that society see these new relationships as just as normal and valuable as the historically constant, culturally universal, and socially normative married heterosexual family. One is to be seen as no better, more important, or necessary than another. Isn't this exactly where we are today? And this moment has no parallel in history.

Consider what happens to someone if they publicly express even polite dissent of such things. We read of such instances quite regularly and they are neither pretty nor civil. What happened in the Chick-fil-A incident in 2012—after its CEO spoke out in favor of traditional marriage—was a dramatic example of this new phenomenon. Unfortunately, no one from the LGBT community as far as I can find offered any public apology for the vicious intolerance, threats of violence, and name-calling hurled at the owners and employees of that company—and simply because one of the owners expressed his support for the natural family.

> It is important to be honest: both sides of this issue have acted very unkindly and irresponsibly toward one another.

However, in the Christian community there are those who also use abuse, spewing very foul names when referring to same-sex-attracted people; they don't hesitate to say things about gay and lesbian people and practices that are just not true. If one is going to make an accusation about another, as in any part of life, you better know what you're talking about. To speak falsely against someone is addressed in one of those Ten Commandments.

But at the same time, does this mean one should never speak critically of another? No genuine relationship operates that way. But make sure you are being both true and fair in such criticisms.

It is important to understand and be honest about the fact that both sides of this issue have acted very unkindly and irresponsibly toward one another. Neither side alone holds the prize for incivility and nastiness. But of course, this should compel us as the church to do even better than we have. Our obedience to Christ's command to love—not only our neighbor but those who persecute us—is not dependent upon how our "enemies" conduct themselves. It is to be unconditional.

A Great Challenge—and Opportunity

So as we face this unique development in our lifetime—providing both challenges and opportunities—we have no real past to look back upon to see exactly how our forefathers dealt with it. God, in His infinite and sometimes hard-to-follow wisdom, has ordained that we be the ones on the stage of His church at this time. We are the mothers and fathers of the faith that coming generations will look back upon. Will they look back at us in admiration and appreciation or disdain and disappointment for how we lived out and passed on our common faith in our age? I think it comes down to whether we lived in both grace and truth.

Now is the time to determine which that will be. Now is the time to meet the unique challenge of this day in fidelity to God's calling, in fidelity to His undying and overflowing heart for all people, we who are that prodigal son or daughter.

This book is written with great humility and some small measure of experience—learned through many missteps and mistakes—in how to meet such a challenge in a faithful and God-honoring way, primarily by learning from the example of those brothers and sisters today who are practicing it well in real life. It is a well-worn phrase among Christians, but no less applicable: "And who knows whether [we] have not come to the kingdom for such a time as this?" (Esther 4:14).

The fact that we *are* indeed here at such a time as this answers the question. This book is all about helping us prepare to fully understand and faithfully meet this important challenge in grace and truth, in boldness and compassion. It is both a time of challenge and opportunity.

So, in short, this book...

(1) is not a book to explain why homosexuality is wrong and how people who are same-sex-attracted must be condemned for what they do.

(2) But neither is it a "Can't-we-just-all-get-along" kumbaya kind of book seeking to put our differences aside and just focus on what can bring us together. To do this is not to deal with the issue and those involved in it honestly and therefore respectfully. There are plenty of books like that if you feel that is what you need.

This is a book about how to live, as much as possible, lovingly and honestly in the essential balance of grace and truth with those who identify themselves with the LGBT community and movement. These two must always go together, for they balance out and sharpen each other. Truth without grace is abusive and grace without truth is mere sentimentalism. The two cannot exist without each other.

And we must walk in this balance in the spirit of Christ our Lord. That is what we are called to in this age.

1

UNDERSTANDING THE THING ITSELF

One of the first realities in dealing intelligently with an issue is to be able to separate the truth undergirding that issue from the fiction and assumption that swirls so speciously around it.

If one doesn't know the truth concerning the basic issues, you can't really know the larger issues. For instance, some otherwise intelligent people hold some ideas about Christianity, and particularly evangelicals, that are simply false. Therefore, they begin from the wrong starting place in their interactions with evangelical Christians, regardless of how confidently they might assert or believe those ideas. Some militant atheists will do this, building a straw-man god and then explaining how unreasonable it is to believe in such a god. It creates the kind of situation that compelled Richard John Neuhaus to respond to one of the more famous atheist gadflies, "The God that you don't believe in is not the God I believe in." We don't want to be that guy.

When I speak on secular campuses on issues like the politics of gender, one of my favorite things is to go out to dinner afterward with the event's hosts, usually the campus's LGBT groups. I like this time because it allows us the opportunity to be able to mix and chat without the official "professionalism" required for the event itself. We can let our hair down a bit. I usually start by breaking the ice, inviting them to ask me any questions they are curious about regarding evangelical faith and practice. After all, I tell them, "When will you ever get a chance to grill someone from the evil empire of the religious right?" And I tell them there's no question that I've not been asked before or will offend me, so have at it. This openness and self-deprecation helps put them at ease and opens things up.

In these exchanges over chicken wings or quesadillas at the local Applebee's, I often hear some variation of this setup to a question: "So as someone who takes the Bible literally..." I stop them and inform them that, in fact, I do not take the Bible literally. They look surprised, as if I had said some vegetarians love a good all-beef hot dog now and then. And then I add, "Actually, no Christian group has ever taken the Bible literally." They look even more flabbergasted and wonder if I am playing some kind of clever mind game with them. I explain to them that I assume what they actually mean is "As someone who takes the Bible seriously, as trustworthy and authoritative..." and they explain that is precisely what they meant.

> We can't talk thoughtfully and productively about what we don't understand.

I then explain to them that even the most hyperconservative of Christians realize that the Bible includes statements of literal fact— "no one comes to the Father but by me"—but also allegory and allusion such as another of Jesus' statement that "you must be born again." He is not talking about literally going back into one's mother's womb, and no Christian has ever taken it as such. He uses it as illustration of a larger truth. And then I get to explain what Jesus meant by it.

It is a good and meaningful opportunity to set such misunderstandings aright. And we should not settle for the same kinds of popularly held but false notions about others. We should seek to understand them correctly.

In fact, one day on one of our many road trips to a debate at some college, I asked my regular debate partner to help me understand the different subcommunities of the larger gay male community, the leather boys, the western rodeo guys, the interior design/fashion chaps. We talked about that for some while and then I asked him what kind of community there was among African-Americans. He asked if he had ever told me about the time he had gone to a Black gay bar. I would have remembered such a story, as my friend going to such a place would be like Mr. Rogers going to a monster truck rally—a fish-out-of-water kind of thing. It promised to be a great story, and he told it with relish.

This particular bar, all the way over on "the other side of town," had a large, muscular man watching the door, and all had to pass by him to get in. As my buddy approached, this large fellow looked at him and then reached out his arms to each side, just above his waist. My friend thought, "Wow, they are friendlier here than most bars I go to," thinking the man wanted to welcome him with a warm inviting hug. Of course, he went to return the kindness and hugged him. His guide that night, a local, informed him that the guard was trying to pat him down for firearms, not welcoming him with physical tenderness. So, as was the moral of my friend's story, sometimes the different parts of the gay community are not so easy to figure out, just as in any community. And now I know and you do too: gun safety is paramount at Black gay bars.

We need to understand some things about the community we are interested in reaching out to, as no one can have an intelligent and accurate conversation or disagreement if it's based on misunderstanding and stereotype, right? To do so is to "dance on Vaseline," as one of David Byrne's songs would have it. You can never make any real connection with the stability of the floor. We can't talk thoughtfully and productively about what we don't understand. And the fault is not in not knowing the facts and truth about something, for not one of us can understand everything accurately. The fault lies in assuming and acting like we do.

Like any complex issue, this one is loaded with nuance and legitimate differences of interpretation and opinion. Take for instance an example from our own community: the issue of infant baptism. On which side of this topic does the truth reside? To which conviction do most Christians adhere? We might each *think* we know, for it probably corresponds with the position we hold. But there is no black-and-white answer. Faithful, biblical Christians line up on both sides of this issue. And so it is with the complexities of LGBT identity. As we unpack these issues, I will try to be sensitive to nuance and I will as best I can seek to separate falsity from fact. And I will strive to do so based on generally agreed upon understandings from serious leaders on various sides of this topic.

These are very important ground markers to be mindful of as we start our journey through the natural thickets of this issue. Bottom line: *We can't get right what we don't understand.*

What's LGBT, Anyway?

It is the rare person who has not heard these four letters as a social and political representation in society today. But what do they mean and how do they relate to one another, or not? First, the letters themselves and their popular meaning:

L—*Lesbian*, women who are sexually attracted to other women.
G—*Gay*, men who are sexually attracted to other men. However, "gay" can also be used as a general term to denote same-sex attraction as in "gay rights" or "gay pride."
B—*Bisexual*, one who is sexually attracted to and interested in both male and female. (It is curious that while the foundational truth of queer and gender theory is that the "binary" understanding of gender—there is only male and female—is

completely false, the "B" here assumes a binary understanding of gender, does it not?)

T—*Transgendered*, a person who was physically born male or female, but is either starting the transition to or currently lives according to the gender that they feel they really are inside. (Here as well, we tend to see the binary essence of gender at work as nearly all transgendered people are described and understood within the community as either "MTF" [male-to-female] or "FTM" [female-to-male] transgendered.)

But while it is typical that these four letters are used, often a few other designations are assumed and sometimes added to this string of four letters, such as . . .

Q or QQ—for either *queer* or/and *questioning*. "Queer" is an imprecise term that can be a political, attitudinal, or generally philosophical term. It generally identifies one as challenging the moral value and hierarchy of most sexual expressions and identities; kind of a sexual anarchism, if you will. But it can mean different things to different people, even within the LGBT community.

During a debate at Otterbein University in Ohio some years ago, our faculty moderator for the event introduced herself officially to the audience as "Queer Straight." Afterward I asked my opponent, who is a noted leader in the LGBT movement (i.e., he knows his stuff), what "queer straight" meant. His answer? "Beats me!" he said. And it wasn't because he hadn't been paying attention in class. It's that many use these terms in very fluid ways. So there are no hard-and-fast rules, black-and-white, dictionary-type understandings about what some terms used in this community actually mean. And "queer" is one of them for the most part.

"Questioning" is simply that. It denotes someone who is still trying to figure themselves out sexually and gender-wise. (Closely related, a "C" can also be added to this train of letters denoting one being "curious" about other kinds of sexual natures and behaviors.)

But there are other letters added to these more often used ones. They are:

> **I**—*Intersexed* is a newer term for hermaphrodite, one who was born with ambiguous genitalia or chromosomal issues that don't distinguish one clearly as either male or female. The intersexed are much less likely to be politically or socially active about their condition compared with those who identify with the first five letters. They will nearly always come to identify exclusively as either male or female. It is also the most medically objective, measurable, and observable of any of these other identities. Except for the chromosomal abnormality, it nearly always reveals itself remarkably early, usually right at birth. It is more a physiological issue than a perception of one's self.

> **A**—*Asexual* is simply that: one who has no sexual attraction to others or interest in sexual activity at all. Curiously, they are seldom active in or a part of this community of which everyone else is identified by their sexuality. It's like being in a boat club and neither having a boat or being interested in boats. Most, like the intersexed, tend to live privately with their secret, and they prefer it this way.

"LGBT" is not just one thing.

> **A**—*Ally* is typically a heterosexual who is down with the cause, actively standing alongside all the other letters. This is what I first thought the "queer straight" Otterbein professor was describing herself as. Perhaps she was.

So, there you have it. To be as inclusive as you can be today, you want to use the full LGBTQQIAA initials train like they do at Amherst College and many other places.[1]

P for polygamous, however, does not seem to be included in anyone's alphabet soup list. Why it isn't is a good question. Serious people are making serious cases for the acceptance of such people. The same goes for another P—*polygamy*. Or you could include others who genuinely advocate for inclusion: pansexual, omnisexual, tri-sexual, agender, bi-gender, third gender, transvestite, polyamorous, undecided, and then the catch-all category: *other*. As I write this, Facebook just added new gender/sexual orientation categories to their binary male/female options in one's personal profile. How many did they add? Over fifty! And users are still complaining their kind has been left out. It's crazy out there, folks, and in using such terms genuine inclusion is literally impossible. It's worth noting that the LGBT community itself includes no small number of those who poke fun at the ever-increasing string of letters that strive for absolute inclusion of every possibility. They prefer it simple: *just be who you are*.

All this is important to know because the "LGBT" initializing does not just mean one is gay or lesbian or even that you are a particular, concise *something*. It does not and cannot refer to who a person is. As my friend John Corvino—one of my longest-standing and dearest friends in the LGBT community—explains in the *New York Times*, "I'm amused whenever I hear someone say 'as an LGBT person...' *Nobody* is an LGBT person. You can have two, maybe three letters maximum at any moment (three could be a bisexual trans man in a gay relationship). It's a little better to say, 'As a member of the LGBT community...'"[2]

---

1. A helpful article on this growing string of letters and in using such terms is: Michael Schulman, "Generation LGBTQIA," *New York Times*, January 9, 2013.
2. John Corvino, "The Two Variables Don't Always Intersect," *New York Times*, December 17, 2013.

One Big Happy Family?

LGBT is not just one thing. It is not a personal descriptor. It is not a manner of being but a social and political identity. It communicates identification with a broad range of alternative sexual and gender norms, a shorthand for a large group of generally similar people who are different. It is much like the term "evangelical," which is not a specific, objective thing. It is a sense of being and an identifier.

So to say that one is supportive of LGBT rights requires some clarification. Would they be for the rights of *all* alternative sexual/gender forms or just a few of those included in the ever-growing letters that make up this expanding community? It is not an academic point, as it would be a minority in the LGBT community who would advocate for the specific "rights" of all the various sexual identities in this ever-expanding alphabet soup. Equal rights for asexuals, the questioning or the curious—What does that even mean? So, to the question of whether you support or oppose LGBT rights, the honest answer for even those within the LGBT community is "it depends."

This is also because the LGBT community itself struggles with this. They are not one big happy family. The "Ls" and the "Gs" have their serious issues with each other and they both have their issues with the "Ts." One very blunt leader in the LGBT movement observes the inherent inequity that can exist there: "The gay establishment has always taken 'L.G.B.T.' to mean gay, with lesbian in parentheses, throw out the bisexuals, and put trans on for a little bit of window dressing."[3]

There are disagreements about who should and should not be permitted to participate in gay-pride parades.[4] Lesbians, self-identified "dykes," and the transgendered will often take their ball and go form

---

3. Matilda Bernstein Sycamore, "A Movement That's a Little More Radical," *New York Times*, October 15, 2013.
4. See Chelsea Kilpack, "The Invisible LBT in Gay Pride," June 1, 2013 at slcfeminist. com; Rev. Dr. Jerry S. Maneker, "The Counterproductive Nature of Parades," n.d. at whosoever.org.

their own events, knowing they are often not welcome.

One significant instance of deliberate internal exclusion regards some policies of the Human Rights Campaign (HRC), arguably the most powerful and influential LGBT advocacy organization in the world. Mainstream gay publications have reported on their controversial history up to the present of questioning whether, ironically, transgendered citizens should even be included in certain federal bills favoring LGBT citizens or whether they should be permitted to protest as "Ts" at important political LGBT rallies. They get excluded because their presence makes for bad TV footage on the evening news.

Full inclusion of transgendered issues in the LGBT movement's efforts have also been either questioned or rejected by majorities in the larger LGBT community in the recent past.[5] So the "T" in LGBT should more accurately be referred to as "Y" as in the vowels: "LGB . . . and sometimes T."[6] As well, the "Bs" are sometimes chided with encouragement from the "Ls" and "Gs" to, for crying out loud, "make a decision and pick a side!"

All this is not presented as a criticism of this movement, for very few movements walk in lockstep with its various constituencies. But knowing that the LGBT community is not one monolithic bloc does help us understand it more honestly. It is truly not *one* thing. In like manner, many outside the evangelical community see us as all happily walking along in total agreement on every important topic, but we know all too well that is not true. The charismatics are nutty, the Reformed think they know everything, the nondenominationals have serious commitment issues, and what's up with those Wesleyans?

Talking with my gay and lesbian friends about these internal dis-

---

5. See Sunnivie Brydum, "Will Trans Folk Become an ENDA Bargaining Chip?" *The Advocate*, November 8, 2013 at advocate.com; Sunnivie Brydum, "HRC and Coalition Apologize for Silencing Undocumented, Trans Activists at Supreme Court," April 1, 2013, at advocate.com and "More Details Obtained about HRC's ENDA Poll," November 10, 2007, at advocate.com.
6. "Are 'Trans Rights' and 'Gay Rights' Still Allies?" *New York Times*, October 15, 2013.

agreements and differences has made for many revealing, long-into-the-night conversations. It has surprised both of us to learn who gets along swimmingly with whom in our communities, and who would never want to be stuck in an elevator with whom and why. But as we consider loving our LGBT neighbors, it is actually the first step in being loving to honestly understand who they are and what they are about. Holding on to unfounded assumptions and misunderstandings can be disrespectful. This is an important point that leads us in to our next topic of understanding.

Homosexuality: What It Is and Isn't

To ask what homosexuality is seems like a silly question, right? *Uh, Glenn, can we move on to the advanced class?*

Bottom line, it is sexual attraction to someone of the same sex. But there are important distinctions that need to be made here in order for us to fully understand what it is and what it isn't, both today and in the recent past. Homosexuality, as we understand it, has undergone a profound evolution over the ages.

Homosexuality existed in relatively widespread ways in the ancient world. But it was much, much different in its social practice and understanding than today. One leading scholar of Greco-Roman sexual mores explains:

> In the ancient world, sanctionable homosexual acts were usually based on inequity: you are not supposed to desire somebody of the same age and status category as yourself. Therefore, young men and slaves are fair game, particularly your own slaves, who are your passive human property.[7]

---

7. Dominic Montserrat, *Sex and Society in Greco-Roman Egypt* (London: Kegan Paul International, 1996), 137–38.

These "sanctionable" relationships are about power and objectification, not caring, respect, and mutual love.

Michel Foucault, in his three-volume *History of Sexuality*, explains that "homosexuality" as a physiological or psychological category was not even present in the minds or language of the ancient or even premodern worlds. It was not how one was but an action, something one did. He explains,

> The enjoyment of boys and of women did not constitute two classificatory categories between which individuals could be distributed [gay or straight]; a man who preferred *paidika* [sex with boys, which was the most common form of same-sex sex apart from with slaves] did not think of himself as being different from those who pursued women.[8]

David Halperin, noted for his groundbreaking work in the area of sexuality in antiquity, agrees, holding that "homosexuality" as a category for understanding or identifying oneself is just about a century old.[9] In fact, the word only came into use in the later 1800s. Prior to that, it went by different terms, even by those who were deeply favorable to sexual experimentation.

The leading, earliest, and most liberal sexologist of that time—Henry Havelock Ellis, writing at the turn of the last century—referred to same-sex sexual activity as "sexual inversion." The German radical Magnus Hirschfeld, around the same time, referred to men who had sex with other men as "intermediates." The term "homosexual" only came into general use and understanding through the early decades of the 1900s.

But at that time, it was largely understood as an act someone did

8. Michel Foucault, *The History of Sexuality*, vol. 2: *The Use of Pleasure* (New York: Vintage Books, 1990), 190.
9. David M. Halperin et al., *Before Sexuality: Construction of the Erotic Experience in the Ancient Greek World* (Princeton, NJ: Princeton University Press, 1990).

to or with another. Later it came to be understood as a psychological disorder for which one needed treatment. Only recently, since the mid-1970s, was it ever referred to as an "orientation" rather than a mere act or a mental condition.

And since the mid-80s to early 90s, it came to be known as one's identifying characteristic, if they so wished. So homosexuality's social evolution has been to date:

- An act
- To a thing in itself, classified as a disorder to be healed of
- To an orientation and thus, a political movement
- To an identity, and thus, a right

All this happened within the last hundred years or so and make up what has ultimately become gay culture. It has become so distinct and prominent that it is not hard for most people to miss identifying it, and intentionally so.

Attraction, Orientation, and Identity

Two of the smartest, most balanced scholars studying the nature of homosexuality in the evangelical community are Stanton Jones and Mark A. Yarhouse. But they are also widely respected by their peers outside evangelicalism. They explain an important distinction between three things we typically see as one and the same: sexual attraction, sexual orientation, and sexual identity. What would you say the difference is, if anything?

They explain that according to the best available research on sexuality in America, conducted at the University of Chicago, individuals who report having same-sex *attraction* make up 4 to 6 percent of the total US population, females and males respectively. This can mean various levels or consistency of such attraction from "rarely" to "sometimes" to "usually" to "always." It would be those who "always" experience same-sex attraction who would be said to have a same-sex sexual *orientation*, what their consistent or strongly dominant sexual desire or preference is. Regarding *identity*, Jones and Yarhouse explain, "Among these [who are oriented as same-sex-attracted], an even smaller percentage self identifies as gay or lesbian, that is, they take on the sociocultural identity as 'gay.'"[10]

Same-sex *identity* is a subset of *orientation* is a subset of *attraction* like nesting dolls, with the first being a smaller part of the next, or three larger-to-smaller parts of a pyramid.

One who is same-sex-attracted might not necessarily consider himself homosexual. Or they might. But he or she who has an orientation or even identity are very likely to consider themselves homosexual. But not all who have an attraction in that way necessarily have identity per se. It is also important to recognize that "orientation" is à less precise term than either "attraction" or "identity."

What Is "Orientation"?

"Sexual orientation" as a category of understanding one's sexuality is both very new and very imprecise. There is no scientific model, consistent

---

10. Stanton Jones and Mark A. Yarhouse, *Ex-Gays: A Longitudinal Study of Religiously Mediated Change in Sexual Orientation* (Downers Grove, IL: InterVarsity Press Academic, 2007), 32.

academic understanding or agreement on what it is and is not. Jones and Yarhouse explain: "We often use the terms *heterosexual, homosexual,* and *bisexual* to communicate information about a person's sexual orientation. Interestingly, there remains much debate among human sexuality experts as to what sexual orientation actually *is.*"[11]

"Orientation" is generally and narrowly defined as what gender one is sexually attracted to. But some argue that it should include how *many* one is attracted to as well as how that attraction is demonstrated sexually.

Is bisexuality really an orientation or merely a lack of having one's feet planted squarely in the hetero- or homosexual camp? Is asexuality an orientation or the absence of one? People disagree on whether it is or not. Is polyamory (having many lovers simultaneously) an orientation? Few in the LGBT community would say so, but the polyamorists believe it most certainly is. Is polygamy an orientation, nonmonogamy, or pedophilia? How about S&M? There are those who intelligently argue that each of these are all orientations, even if they disagree with their ethical value. Others are more exclusive in what is and is not an orientation.

The answer, however, is that no one can say for sure, because there are no distinct lines or scientific criteria for what makes one sexual preference or attraction an "orientation" and another not.

It is not a useless term but an imprecise one. And the question of whether one's orientation is innate or a natural part of who they are is another important question that we will address in chapter 3.

Are All Homosexuals Gay?

This question is not as obvious as you may think. Nor is it a trick question.

---

11. Ibid., 29.

I often make the seemingly outlandish claim in my talks that not all homosexuals are gay. The audience wonders if I'm referencing some contradictory Taoist truism, like "The further one travels, the closer one gets to home." Or I might mean that some homosexuals are just pretending to be homosexual or perhaps, that some same-sex-attracted people refuse to act on their sexual attractions. It's like saying "not all walkers are pedestrians," right? But I am making a serious, factual, and meaningful point that we must appreciate. It is what Jones and Yarhouse stated above.

Homosexuality speaks of attraction and in many ways can refer to a personal identity. Gay is something beyond this, a sociopolitical, ideological distinctive. It is more of an attitude, if you will, generally signifying "I'm all in for the cause." We might make comparable distinctions among a gun owner, a gun enthusiast, and a lifetime member of the NRA. Although similar, each of these speaks of different levels of commitment to an ideal. They are very different kinds of people.

When I think of the difference between homosexual and gay, I think about my parents' longtime next-door neighbors, Sondra and Nia.

Lesbians in their later fifties, they are generally a conservative and quiet couple. Nia works for the city as a customer relations manager in the water and sanitation department. Sondra is a legal assistant in a large law office. Would they consider themselves same-sex-attracted? *Obviously*. Lesbian? *Probably*. Gay? *Not at all*. They don't have an advocacy bone in their body. They are not "joiners" or movement types. They just see themselves as "us," Sondra and Nia, two partners who love each other and have built a comfortable and quiet life together. They would tell you that not all same-sex-attracted people are gay. Many, if not most, are simply same-sex-attracted people trying to live their lives, work hard, and be happy.

Conclusion

These are all important factors to understand because it is both loving and respectful to seek to understand the nuances, differences, and distinctions of those we want to learn to love well. Nor do we want to mistakenly understand these issues relative to the way they are portrayed and understood in the general culture. There can often be a significant contrast between what real life is like and how it gets portrayed in the general cultural conversation. We don't want to be a variation of those who assume that all conservative Christians take the Bible literally or that all good Christian women are only "speak-when-spoken-to" servants of their husbands.

We owe it to those we want to befriend to seek to understand them and their community as best we can. And we should be willing and eager to help them understand ours, if they so desire, explaining truthfully that we are not all like *this* or like *that*. All communities are more complex on the inside than they appear, and it's honoring to work to understand that complexity.

We are individuals seeking to live out our faith; they are individuals trying to live in line with their sexual interests. We don't appreciate being lumped in with a stereotype and neither do they. We all want to be seen, understood, and hopefully accepted for who we are.

2

SEX: WHAT IS IT THAT GOD SAYS?

What would you think of a Darwinist who wasn't really sure of Darwin's thoughts on important issues related to Darwinism? Would a Marxist who didn't know Marx's basic teachings on humanity be a respectable Marxist? What about an avid fan of a celebrity personal trainer not knowing what he had to say about smoking, refined sugar, yoga, or a low-carb diet? They wouldn't really be true students, would they?

Christians can be like this when it comes to our faith and its teachings. We must know, or at least learn, what our Lord said on many important topics if we are to call ourselves serious and faithful followers. Good Christians should know what Jesus said about whether it is better to travel by donkey or by walking. Okay, that's a trick statement. It clearly wasn't in His mission (or interest) to speak on such things. He gave no direction on whether an omelet should be made with egg whites or whole eggs or whether men should wear hats or not. Those are areas where we are free to determine what is best with the good wisdom and insight He blessed us with.

But, of course, there are things He spoke clearly and definitively on, such as money, the Devil, the religious leaders of the day, His Father, the character of a good person, or what eternity is like. A good Christian who has some years under her belt should know that He had much to say on these topics and others and what those things are. A good servant knows what his master wants and demands. And he also desires and seeks to obey it.

In an increasingly sexualized culture, with all kinds of competing values coming at us and our children from nearly all quarters, we must know what it is that Christ said about sexuality and His desire for us regarding this important part of our God-created humanity. He didn't speak about it a great deal, but what He did say was direct, clear, and concise. And it is a significantly important subject to God because it is such a central part of what He made us to be as male and female.

So what did Jesus say concerning our sexuality?
To bottom line it, He said these things:

- Quoting from the first two chapters of Genesis, He declares that God created man male and female, each for the other, and the man is to leave his mother and father and give himself totally to his wife, and she to him. And in this marital union, they become one flesh. This marital and sexual union is to be exclusive and should not be broken by anyone. (See Matthew 19:4–6; Mark 10:6–9.)
- To the woman caught in a sexual relationship with a man who was not her husband, He said, "Neither do I condemn you; go, and from now on sin no more" (John 8:11).
- It is not enough not to commit adultery; there is a harder line. Even to look lustfully at another commits that sin in one's heart, Jesus explained. And whatever causes you to sin, make sure you deal with it swiftly and decisively because the consequences are serious! (See Matthew 5:27–30.)

- To a Samaritan woman He met at Jacob's Well one day, He brought up the topic of her husband, how she had had five husbands and the man she was with now was not her husband. He was concerned about this. She knew it and quickly tried to change the subject. (See John 4:16–18.)

Is it unfounded to say that Jesus tells us that the human sexual relationship is created to be between a husband and a wife? It is not for those who really love one another, even *really, really* love one another! It is not for those who want to test each other out first, to see if there is compatibility. It is not for those who have moved in together. It is not for those who want to have a baby together. *The sexual union is the marital union.* And all other kinds are *sinful,* an unfashionable word but the Lord Himself used it quite often. If that is too narrow for your liking, take it up with God. I myself would lobby for changing the "has already committed adultery . . . in his heart" from Matthew 5:28 to "adultery in actuality." It's a tough one and sometimes doesn't make me feel good about myself. And sometimes I am guilty of committing adultery by this measure. But guess what? That's the way it is, right?

> In an increasingly sexualized culture, we must know what Christ said about sexuality.

The church has not questioned this truth on Christianity's sexual ethics at any time since its inception. In fact, the early church, just like today, caused quite a stir over its firm monogamous, exclusive-to-marriage sexual ethic of mutual respect and care. The only option for those who are set on changing or rewriting this ethic is to found their own new faith.

Below are excerpts from an important piece by Eve Tushnet in which she reflects on how she reconciles being a lesbian with her obedience to the teaching of her church on sexuality. The entire piece is well worth the read and can be found through the footnote below.[1]

[My] sheltered upbringing may help explain my sunny undergraduate confidence that even though I knew of literally nobody else who had ever tried to be both unashamedly gay and obediently Catholic, I was totally going to do it. No problem, guys, I got this . . .

Things look different now. I hope I've learned a few things about the dangers of sophomoric self-confidence: There are times when my relationship with the Catholic Church feels a lot like Margaret Atwood's ferocious little poem,

> You fit into me
> like a hook into an eye
> a fish hook
> an open eye

And I've met many other gay or queer or same-sex-attracted Christians, in all flavors of Christianity. I have several friends in same-sex marriages now, including one who had an Episcopalian church wedding with all the trimmings. I also have many friends who, like me, are trying to live in accordance with the historical Christian teaching on chastity, including its prohibition on sex between men or between women.

. . . Many Christian churches are beginning to integrate gay marriage into their theology. Their preexisting theology—not

---

1. Eve Tushnet, "I'm Gay, but I'm Not Switching to a Church That Supports Gay Marriage," May 30, 2013, http://www.theatlantic.com/sexes/archive/2013/05/im-gay-but-im-not-switching-to-a-church-that-supports-gay-marriage/276383/.

only on marriage but on creation, embodiment, and Scriptural interpretation—has begun to shift to match the new unisex or gender-neutral model of marriage. With so many more options for gay Christians, why stick with the fishhook?

The biggest reason I don't just de-pope myself is that I fell in love with the Catholic Church. Very few people just "believe in God" in an abstract way; we convert, or stay Christian, within a particular church and tradition. I didn't switch from atheistic post-Judaism to "belief in God," but to Catholicism: the Incarnation and the Crucifixion, Michelangelo and Wilde, St. Francis and Dorothy Day. I loved the church's beauty and sensual glamour.

. . . But I do think it was okay to enter the church without being able to justify all of her teachings on my own. The true answer was that I didn't understand the teaching [on homosexuality], but had agreed to accept it as the cost of being Catholic. To receive the Eucharist I had to sign on the dotted line . . . and I longed intensely for the Eucharist, so I figured, everybody has to sacrifice something. God doesn't promise that He'll only ask you for the sacrifices you agree with and understand.

Right now, the Biblical witness seems pretty clear. Both opposite-sex and same-sex love are used, in the Bible, as images of God's love. The opposite-sex love is found in marriage—sexually exclusive marriage, an image which recurs not only in the Song of Songs but in the prophets and in the New Testament—and the same-sex love is friendship. Both of these forms of love are considered real and beautiful; neither is better than the other. But they're not interchangeable. Moreover, Genesis names sexual difference as the only difference which was present in Eden. There were no racial differences, no age difference, no children and therefore no parents. Regardless of how literally you want to take the creation narratives, the Bible sets apart sexual difference as a uniquely profound form of difference. Marriage, as the union of man and woman, represents communion with the Other in a way which makes it an especially powerful image of the way we can commune with the God who remains Other. That's a quick and dirty summary, but it seems to me more responsive to the texts, more willing to defer to historical Christian witness, and more attuned to the importance and meaning of our bodies than most of the defenses I've read of Christian gay marriage.

But being embedded in Catholicism colors my reading of the Bible—that is actually what tradition is supposed to do—and shapes my sense of which elements of Christian history are essential and which are wanderings from the path. So the main reason I'm planning on celibacy for the foreseeable future is just that I'm Catholic and lesbian and them's the rules, bud.

In the Beginning . . .

It is important to see that Jesus, in the first bullet above (Matthew 19 and Mark 10), takes His audience who asked Him about marital and sexual relationships to the very beginning of God's creation. He quotes from Genesis 1 and 2 about how God created mankind in a dual humanity as male and female, for each other and for marriage. Jesus is affirming the truth and wisdom of the original creation story, which some tend to dismiss as mere allegory or such, even though Genesis 1:26–27 declares that humanity is made in God's very image and likeness. And in this image, God created them male and female. Those are the only two models He produces.

> Two people of the same sex cannot become one flesh, no matter how much they love each other.

This duality means something truly remarkable about being human: the male represents the image of God in his unique way and the female represents the image of God in her unique way. Neither can do that for the other. And then in Genesis 1:28, God calls them to their first task: to come together as husband and wife and begin a family, bringing forth new, eternal God-imagers. They are made for this by God's very design and more importantly, His delight.

And Jesus, in His explanation, also makes reference to the creation narrative in Genesis 2:23–24 where He reiterates that as God made them male and female, it is God's will that the man leave his mother and father and cling to, hold fast to, cleave to his wife. This essentially means that the man will put his wife before all other relationships, even that with his own mother and father. And through their marital and sexual union, they will become one flesh.

An unmarried man and woman cannot become one flesh as God intended, regardless of how much they love one another, how "right" they seem for each other, or how hot their sex is. It is only the marital union and embrace that create this ontological mystery and miracle of physics. Two people of the same sex cannot become one flesh, no matter how much they love one another or how long they have been together, because their union does not bring the two different types of God-imagers together to create a fuller divine and human picture of what humanity is. When a husband and wife come together, it is a different and higher proclamation that is both divine and human than when any other two come together, gay or straight.

It Is Not Good . . .

God explained to us in Genesis 2:18 that it is not good for man to be alone. This is the most profound statement about our humanity in all of literature, second only to the statement that we are created in God's image. It says something so very fundamental and universal about all human beings. And it is not just about loneliness, for man had a direct relationship with God as well as the animals. He had relationships and one very important relationship in particular. So what was God saying?

What God was referring to was human isolation, one from another. Man did not have a human "other." It was not how humanity was created to be as an image-bearer of the triune God who is in Himself a divine family of love, self-giving, and intimacy. And in this image, he didn't just need a fishing buddy or someone to help him with the work around the garden but a mate. He needed someone like him in his humanness, but very different from him in his maleness. And we all know what the solution to the problem of man's original and existential solitude was. It is finally at this point in creation that humanity fully images God.

Throughout Scripture as well as Jewish and Christian history, there is no other sexual or marital relationship outside the married man and woman union that bears God's blessing and approval. This is evident and undeniable. And it is not just because that was the "old" way of looking at things. The creation story was *very* old in Jesus' time, and He did not try to modernize it for His time but strongly affirmed it as authoritative and directive regarding what we should believe and how we should conduct ourselves.

There is no indication any of this is up for debate in our Lord's eyes.

So, to sum up: It is male and female who show forth the image of God in the world, and each does so in ways the other cannot. And it is in their union and communion that humanity truly becomes whole, what God intended it to be, for when Adam was alone, God said it was not good. The sexual union is the husband and wife marital union. Anything else is not an option in God's design.

We are all divinely made for the intimacy we get originally from our mother and father, where we flow as a new life from their physical and loving intimacy as man and wife.

And we are all divinely made for the intimacy we grow into in adulthood, most importantly is the intimacy with a spouse who will complete and complement us as our gender-distinct "other," with whom we can hopefully become a loving mother and father with to begin the next cycle of this essential human process.[2]

This is a central and primary part of what it means to be human. As the saying goes, nobody on their deathbed regrets not having spent enough time at work, not having enough boats, a big enough house, cool cars, or a killer dining room set. They regret not being closer to and investing more in their family.

Now think about this important question: *If male and female are both the unique image and likeness of God in the world, how would Satan best attack God's image and likeness in the world, something to which he is egotistically obsessed with?*

He would try to convince us that male and female have no real unique meaning, importance, or familial or social necessity because he *knows* better than all of us what this represents. He's a brilliant theologian, as he knows the nuances and important points of the story quite well. And this questioning, let alone outright dismissal, is happening today in large parts of academia, the arts, and media. As one celebrated professor of sociology working from both Brown and the University of Maryland said at a small academic meeting a colleague was hosting, "Sex difference only matters in the bathroom and the bedroom." And she believed this with every part of her well-educated being. And to many in the room, she was saying nothing controversial. It is more common than not among cultural elites. But would you like to believe that your manhood or womanhood only matters for how you have sex or use the toilet? It's a very reductionist view of humanity.

---

2. This, of course, does not mean that those who are not married or never marry are not complete as God-imagers. But in all human societies, singleness is an exception, and most who are single would desire in the deepest part of their hearts to be married if the possibility presented itself. It takes a very unique person to be content in their singleness throughout life. What is more, each of us is the offspring—the actual flesh and blood oneness—of a mother and father's one-flesh oneness.

Now, this is not to say that all people who question the importance of gender difference have signed up in the work of Satan. We all fall victim to Satan's lies. It happened to that couple who had the remarkable privilege of having God perform their wedding. It has happened to each person since. It happens to me and to you. But this doesn't normalize it. It is still sin, but we must have compassion for all who are blinded by the Evil One. It is well known in Christian tradition that the more holy one becomes, living in closer intimacy with God, the more aware of their sin and its seriousness they become.

But we must realize that Satan's deception of getting us to deny or reject the importance of humanity's being as male and female challenges the very likeness and image of God in creation. This is no small thing, and Satan knows it. Yet this should elicit compassion within us, not anger, toward all those who are misled. That is the heart of Christ.

But Jesus Never Mentioned Homosexuality

Gene Robinson, the first ordained open and practicing same-sex-attracted bishop in the Episcopal Church, has made much of explaining how God has no problem with "committed, monogamous homosexual relationships" as he qualifies it. In his recent book, *God Believes in Love*, he asks this question, "What does Jesus say about homosexuality?" His answer is as direct as it is brief. Two words: "Absolutely nothing."[3] Period.

Is this true? Well, the answer is actually yes *and* no. But it's not because He was equivocal in any way. It has to do with how one generally interprets a text, known as *hermeneutics*. No, Jesus is never recorded as having uttered a word about "homosexuality." That much is clear and undisputed. But this certainly does not mean that Jesus said "absolutely nothing" about homosexuality. Let's see why.

---

3. Gene Robinson, *God Believes in Love: Straight Talk about Gay Marriage* (New York: Vintage Books, 2013), 83.

First, Bishop Robinson and many others who make such claims know, as does any first-year logic student, that an argument from silence is no argument. It is like a child telling his parents, "Well, you never *said* I couldn't use my finger paints on my bedroom wall."

It happens in real adult life too. True story: A faculty member at a well-known and widely respected Christian university in California decided she would now live as a man and all that goes along with that. She announced this decision, and the leadership of the school, after long and thoughtful deliberation and discussion with the theology professor, decided to cancel her teaching contract. She said this response surprised her because university policy was silent about faculty changing from one gender to another. *Seriously?*

Arguments from silence are not credible. Jesus never said anything about not stiffing your waitress on her tip either, but other things He said about how to treat people can make us pretty sure He's not keen on it. Putting things together that *were* said to come to a reasonable conclusion about something that was technically never mentioned is credible.

This leads us to the obvious question Robinson and others should ask as a good student of Jesus: *What did He say about sexual ethics in general?*

To that question we have to say that Jesus does indeed say something about homosexuality in His "Haven't you heard from the beginning..." statements we saw above in Matthew 19 and Mark 10. It is here that He clearly and strongly affirms the truth and authority of the original creation narratives that say male and female are the two types of God-imagers in the world and that He made them for each other to become a fuller image of God in their union, as He tells us that it is not good that they be alone. And this is the only sexual relationship that God has given to mankind with both His delight and approval. And this is precisely what Jesus was saying in referring us to the truths taught in Genesis 1 and 2.

So, does Jesus say anything about homosexuality? Of course He does, and someone as well-educated as Robinson should know better. It takes a pretty creative reading to conclude that the Matthew, Mark, or Genesis texts are silent on homosexual sex—or for that matter, unmarried cohabitation, marital infidelity, or unmarried heterosexual sex. And this has not been disputed in over two thousand years of Christianity or much, much longer in Judaism.

Haven't Theologians Shown the Bible Doesn't Condemn Homosexual Sex?

Some theologians have tried to explain by their very careful study of the Scriptures that what the Bible seems to say on sexuality is not actually what it says. They offer some rather creative and innovative examples to explain away the clear meaning of Scripture in such texts as Sodom and Gomorrah and Paul's words in Romans 1.

What is notable is that nearly all of those who revise the widely and long-held understanding of these verses are quite up-front about their self-interest in seeking alternative meanings of these passages as scholars who apply queer-studies hermeneutics to the texts they address. Others admit they have very personal reasons for their new understanding of these texts, often due to having a child or beloved family member come out.

Here is a typical revisionist look at Sodom and Gomorrah:

> Ironically, I believe that these anti-gay Christians actually have it backwards. The true sin of the Sodomites as described in the Bible has nothing to do with same-sex acts per se. Rather, the ancient Sodomites were punished by God for far greater sins: for attempted gang rape, for mob violence, and for turning their backs on strangers and the needy who were in their midst. In other words, the real sin of Sodom was radical inhospitality. [4]

---

4. Rev. Patrick S. Cheng, "What Was the Real Sin of Sodom?" *Huffington Post*, April 20, 2010, http://www.huffingtonpost.com/rev-patrick-s-cheng-phd/what-was-the-real-sin-of_b_543996.html.

Here's an important aside. Note how this revisionist Patrick S. Cheng identifies those who hold the view of homosexuality traditional to Christians, Jews, and Muslims: "anti-gay Christians." It's a slick and manipulative approach: Explain that the belief you are arguing against is held primarily by a sect of unsavory people. What is more, this particular explanation is from a theologian who has also written such books as *Radical Love: An Introduction to Queer Theology* and *From Sin to Amazing Grace: Discovering the Queer Christ*. A unique interpretation of a text is usually suspect when the interpreter has a very personal interest in that interpretation.

Cheng, in line with other such revisionists, contends that God was angry with Sodom because the men of that town didn't welcome Abraham's two visitors in a very nice way. And one is obviously inclined to agree. Every man in town coming to Lot's doorstep trying to power their way in so they can rape his two guests is generally judged inhospitable, even radically so. No argument there. But it is a very novel interpretation to say their sexual intentions had little to do with God's judgment as well.

> Homosexuality as a way of *being* was nonexistent until very recently.

Can they honestly believe that their alternative would have received God's approval? Imagine. "Hello, Lot. We noticed you have two guests staying with you and thought we'd come by to see if they might like to meet some of us and perhaps find any of us sexually desirable. If not, that's fine too. We just want them to feel at home." According to this take on the text all these millennia, all Jews, Christians, and Muslims (not to mention the general culture) thought sodomy was one thing when it's actually something quite different.

What is more, if inhospitality itself is such a grave sin in God's eyes, then why did Bethlehem get a pass? The whole town turned their back on God's own Son on His birthday. *Radical inhospitality* to be sure.

And here's the revisionist take on Romans 1:26–27. When the apostle Paul "seems" to say that men and women traded what is natural for those "dishonorable passions" that are "contrary to nature," he was not speaking of homosexuality per se but something different. They explain that the sin was not that men had sexual passions for men and women for women, but these men and women were acting contrary to their nature because they were heterosexuals and not homosexuals. Thus, it is proper for homosexuals and heterosexuals to act according "to their natures" but not contrary to their sexual natures. It is also contended by these advocates that God's condemnation here is also about the sin of idolatry.

There are many things that need saying here, of course. The first is historical. As we saw in the previous chapter, "homosexuality" as a way of *being* was nonexistent until very recently. Homosexuality was an act and not understood as a thing until the last hundred years or so. And what is more, even today, there is no evidence, scientific or otherwise, that same-sex attraction is rooted solely in one's biology. So there couldn't have been an understanding of a proper "nature" of heterosexuals and one for homosexuals in this text, not then or now.

The second, of course, is the creative reading of Scripture here. Paul is indeed talking about idolatry. They failed to worship God and instead worshiped images of man and animals (Romans 1:23). They were condemned for this and then God gave them over to their "dishonorable passions" (v. 26), which were women desiring women and men consumed with passion for men. As always, idolatry is the chief of all sin and these sexual sins were the consequence in this instance. Paul is telling us the two go together: idolatry gives us over to all other sins. It was the nature of the rebellion of Satan and the disobedience of our original parents. It is what the first command is about and all other sins flow from this: mine, yours, and all others. This is what Paul is saying in Romans, and he is speaking of a specific sin in this instance that came from their idolatry.

Finally, in all my study of the efforts by these various schola..
turn the Scriptures into a pro-gay text, I always find one thing consistently missing. None that I have seen concern themselves with the most important texts on this subject, those that speak to God's actual design for humanity and sexuality. Check it out for yourself. These are found in Genesis 1 and 2 and Jesus' affirmation of these texts in Matthew 19 and Mark 10 as we saw above. It is curious why they would ignore these because they are what is foundational to this question, for they ask, "Why did God create us the way He did as sexual creatures and for what purpose?"

God is unmistakably clear in these texts, and throughout Scripture, about what His gift of sexuality is for and that it is a special male/female communion and life-giving cooperation and union between a husband and wife. If we are going to get a correct interpretation of Scripture as God intended, we have to judge various verses in connection with the fullness of God's Word. This is what reliable and faithful exegesis does.

Fact: Homosexuality Is Not a Sin

"So, if I'm going to hell because I'm a homosexual, then why—" starts the question to me from an art history major at Augustana College at an after-event dinner. I stop her and ask where she got that idea. She seems confused and answers, "Well, isn't that what Christians like you believe?" Not at all, I told her. I like how pastor Tim Keller answers this major misconception: "Homosexuality doesn't send you to hell, any more than heterosexuality sends you to heaven."

I told her that Scripture is unequivocal that we are all afflicted with the cancer of sin that separates us from God. After the fall, hell is the destination of us all, for we are all children of Adam. Our only hope of eternal life with God is to have our sins forgiven through the sacrificial death and saving grace of God's Son, Jesus Christ. This is the first truth of Christianity. We can't be good enough to get there and one's heterosexuality doesn't get him or her to the head of the line and one's homosexuality doesn't send a person to the back of the line. Our sexual orientation certainly doesn't determine our eternal direction.

But, I told her, "The question I think you're getting at is 'Is homosexuality a sin?'" She said it was. "Again, the answer might surprise you," I said.

Being attracted to the same sex is certainly not a sin, just as a man being attracted to a woman he is not married to is not a sin. *But it's what one does with that attraction that matters, just as with any other desire.*

Acting on that desire or attraction, either through lust or sexual activity, is indeed a sin. Taking that attraction and desire, giving it over to God and asking Him to help you live holy in the midst of it is profoundly pleasing to God. Like any good parent, He is eager and willing to help. And He also feels compassion and warmth toward those who want help in such a struggle—as any good parent would.

And it is a sin for both the unmarried heterosexual and the same-sex-attracted person to be sexual with others.[5] Both are called to obedience. As we have seen, the only sexual relationship God desires for us and condones is between a husband and wife. But celibate same-sex attraction, just like celibate heterosexual attraction, is certainly not a sin. And there are many same-sex-attracted Christians who live happy, celibate lives, even though they have their struggles just as unmarried heterosexuals do. And the church needs to encourage them and help them tell their stories so that we don't allow ourselves to live between

---

5. A technical point worth noting: Of course, it is not a sin for a same-sex-attracted person to be in a sexual relationship with his/her opposite-sex spouse. Many are or have been. Gene Robinson, just mentioned, was married to his wife, Isabella, for nearly fifteen years and they had two daughters together. They divorced agreeably when he declared his same-sex attraction. Their sexual relationship as husband and wife was certainly not morally wrong as it followed God's design for marriage.

two false extremes for same-sex-attracted people: "get-delivered-from-your-attraction" vs. "jump-into-the-deep-end-and-embrace-who-you-are-and-all-it-entails." As always, there is reasonable middle ground. Homosexuality is not a sin, just as heterosexuality itself is not a sin. It's what you do with it, though, and the discipline one brings to it with the merciful help of God's Holy Spirit.

It is disobedience that sends us to hell. It was the disobedience of our first father, Adam. And all of us are desperately tainted by his original sin. I am, Billy Graham is, the Pope is, Mother Teresa was. Your pastor is. *It's the great equalizer.* If we understand what the church is from its very beginning, we realize that the only people who can join it are sinners—without exception. Consider Peter, that great rock of faith in the church. Peter denied Christ three times and at a very critical time. Paul, the other great pillar of the church, aggressively persecuted Christ's followers, often to the point of death. In fact, Paul referred to himself as the chief of sinners.

So you and I are in good company, and in the same company with our LGBT friends. But the difference between those going to heaven and those who are not is that some have recognized their disobedience, desired to change it, and then trusted in the only thing that can take our sin away, the grace and sacrificial death of God's Son, Jesus Christ. Heaven is the Christian's future not because of what we do or don't do, but because of what Jesus did for all of us. We place the trust of our lives, for today, for tomorrow, and for eternity in Christ alone.

And temptation is not wrong. Christ was tempted. But it's what we do with it that determines the right or wrong of it. Do we entertain and feed that temptation? Or do we resist it and run into God's protective and rescuing arms? This is a choice that all of us face, homos-, heteros- and all the other kinds of "o's" alike. It is one of the most inclusive things about being human.

Wesley Hill is a young assistant professor of biblical studies, specializing in New Testament, at Trinity School for Ministry. His book, *Washed and Waiting: Reflections on Christian Faithfulness and Homosexuality*, is a concise and deeply honest telling of his struggle as an evangelical and a same-sex-attracted man. A must-read. Through prayer, counseling, therapy, and sheer force of will, he sought freedom from his same-sex attraction, but to no avail. Defecting from his biblically conservative faith to a gay affirming congregation was not an option for him. But neither was denying his sexual desires.

Hill writes honestly about how he's struggled with this dilemma, offering no easy answers. He has decided to remain true to historic Christian teaching—and not just because of where proof-texting took him, as clear as that was. He chooses celibacy for himself because of the larger Christian story of God's actions in redemptive history. He explains:

> Could the Christian story of what God did for the world in Christ be the framework that makes the rules—"Don't go to bed with partners of the same-sex," "Don't seek to cultivate and nurture desires and fantasies of going to bed with a partner of the same sex"—make sense?
>
> . . . In the end, what keeps me on the path that I have chosen is not so much individual proof texts from Scripture or the sheer weight of the church's traditional teaching against homosexual practice. Instead, it is, I think, those texts and traditions and teachings as *I see them from within the true story of what God has done in Jesus Christ*—and the whole perspective on life and the world that flows from that story, as expressed definitively in Scripture . . . I abstain from homosexual behavior because of the power of that scriptural story[6] . . .

---

6. Wesley Hill, *Washed and Waiting: Reflections on Christian Faithfulness and Homosexuality* (Grand Rapids: Zondervan, 2010), 61.

He recognizes that this difficult call to sexual purity is not just for the same-sex attracted: "The message of what God has done through Christ reminds me that all Christians, whatever their sexual orientation, to one degree or another experience the same frustration that I do as God challenges, threatens, endangers, and transforms *all* our natural desires and affections [emphasis his]."[7]

Christian discipleship is a demanding call. Hill, in his book, points us to a passage from Alan Paton's wonderful 1948 novel, *Cry, the Beloved Country*, where its main character, Pastor Kumalo, affirms:

> He paused for a moment, then he said, I do not wish to offend you gentlemen, but the Church too is like the chief. You must do so and so and so. You are not free to have an experience. A man must be faithful and meek and obedient, and he must obey the laws, whatever the laws may be. It is true that the Church speaks with a fine voice . . . [8]

Is Homosexuality a Super-Sin?

At work, among my colleagues, we have a statement that we have to remind ourselves and others of from time to time. It is this, and it has to do with what we just discussed: *There is not a special, hotter place in hell for the homosexual person.*

Certain kinds of disobedience can have different consequences in real life. I have to drive home from a party. I drank too much Scotch and had way too much cake. Gluttony and drunkenness are both sins, but one will have much more serious consequences as I get behind the wheel of my car. But both have the same consequence regarding our relationship with God. Homosexuality is not a super-sin any more than

---

7. Ibid., 64–65.
8. Alan Paton, *Cry, the Beloved Country* (New York: Scribner, 1948, 2003), 32–33.

a number of other things are—seven actually—that God tells us are an abomination in His eyes. (And for the uninitiated, "abomination" means something's pretty bad!)

Proverbs 6:16–19 explains,

> There are six things that the Lord hates, seven that are an abomination to him: haughty eyes, a lying tongue, and hands that shed innocent blood, a heart that devises wicked plans, feet that make haste to run to evil, a false witness who breathes out lies, and one who sows discord among brothers.

Homosexual sex specifically doesn't make this list, but lying does. Pride does. Stirring up trouble between people does. And these are all in the same list with murder. God seems to have a different economy about what are really serious sins than we can tend to have.

Now there are other verses in Scripture that do say that same-sex sexual activity is an abomination.[9] The Bible also seems to state that cross-dressing is an abomination to God.[10] But it also says that

- the devious person,
- a crooked heart,
- lying lips,
- the ways and thoughts of the wicked,
- arrogance and pride of heart,
- unequal weights (cheating and false judgments), and
- the scoffer...

...are all abominations in the eyes of God.[11] It is both a devastating and broad brush painted across all of us. How many of our own actions

---

9. Leviticus 18:22; 20:13.
10. Deuteronomy 22:5.
11. Proverbs 3:32; 11:20; 12:22; 15:9; 16:5; 20:23; 24:9.

and attitudes are not included in this list of abominable sins? Show of hands?

The abomination list is not an exclusive club applicable to only "those people." Membership is free and mandatory when you sign up for humanity. *And none of us has the authority to explain ourselves off the list.*

Now, concerning sexual sin, Scripture says that all sexual sins, for heterosexuals and homosexuals, are different in their nature and consequences from other sins. Paul tells us in 1 Corinthians 6:18 to "Flee from sexual immorality. Every other sin a person commits is outside the body, but the sexually immoral person sins against his own body."

Paul is not telling us that sexual sins are worse sins but that they have different consequences than other sins (as we saw earlier with the sins of gluttony and drunkenness). Both lying and murder are abominations, as we learned above. But lying can be made up for rather quickly with the person we lied to. Murder is a bit more difficult to get over and clean up relationally, if it ever can be. This is what Paul is getting at with sexual immorality. They are sins against our own bodies, and the bodies of others. This tells us that sex is a unique and powerful thing, not to be taken lightly or experimented with. Like fire, it can bring great wonder to our lives in its proper usage. But it can also bring unspeakable devastation when used beyond its proper place.

But just as all of us are condemned for our disobedience toward God, we *all* also have the same hope and opportunity of forgiveness and deliverance from our sin. It is not offered to anyone more than another. Romans 5 tells us: "But God shows his love for us in that while we [collective, not 'they' or 'them'] were still sinners, Christ died for us. For if while we [again, not 'they' or 'them'] were enemies, we were reconciled to God by the death of his Son, much more, now that we are reconciled, shall we be saved by his life" (vv. 8, 10).

> Most engage in sexual sin out of the need for human intimacy.

Sin is serious, deadly serious. And there is no one free from its devastation and damnation: the homosexual and heterosexual of all stripes, the religious and the unbelievers, the wealthy and the poor, the Republican and the Democrat, the supposed "godly" or the "reprobate."

Sin is the great equalizer, just as the grace of God is as well. And we each have a decision to make about which we will allow ourselves to be a slave to. Grace is a much better taskmaster to put oneself under. Its burden is light and ultimately freeing.

The Quest for Human Intimacy

Sexuality is a great gift from God, really the first He gave us, second only to our God-imaging nature. This embrace between a husband and wife is somehow and mystically an image of God Himself and Christ's relationship with His church.[12] As such, it is a very powerful thing and God delights in it for us. When a gift is received in thankfulness and used properly and respectfully in honor of the one who gave it, it delights the Giver. When it is not valued or used in any way contrary to what the Gift-Giver intended, it is an affront to the Giver.

And so it is with sex.

But an important point must be made here. Most engage in sexual sin out of a basic human need God has given and put within them, but that becomes misdirected. And that is not so much the sexual desire but the need for human intimacy. Loneliness and isolation can be the most devastating pain that humans can feel. And we will do many things to free ourselves from that heart-crushing pain.

In a delightful 1945 novel *The World, the Flesh, and Father Smith*, written by a wise and imaginative Scottish writer, Bruce Marshall, we find Miss Agdala, a famous author of erotica, meeting the book's main character on the street as he is on his way to his next appointment. She

---

12. Genesis 1:26–28; Ephesians 5:31–32.

explains to the good Father Smith that she'd "been dying for years to meet a Catholic priest, but somehow there never seem to be any at any of the parties I go to" and that she has just "oodles and oodles to ask you about that I don't know if I'll ever have time." He happily invites her to walk along with him and ask away, and so she does.

As he answers her many questions about the church and sexuality, directly and honestly, she says he has just proved what she had always maintained about the Christian faith, "that religion is only a substitute for sex." Father Smith deftly counters this claim: "I still prefer to believe that sex is a substitute for religion and that the young man who rings the bell at the brothel is unconsciously looking for God."[13]

Father Smith's brilliant observation is as big as it is curious because it helps us see those who stray from God's desire for us with compassion. It also makes a point we must be mindful of as we consider how to love our LGBT neighbors in grace and truth. Each of us are seeking the love we were made for and can only really find in God and His plan for us: the love, acceptance, and intimacy He made us for. And too often, we look for love in all the wrong places. For example,

- The adulterer is looking for that intimacy and acceptance.
- The porn addict is looking for that intimacy and acceptance.
- The young college student who is hooking up is looking for that intimacy and acceptance.
- The man who visits the prostitute is looking for that intimacy and acceptance.
- The married man or woman who lives in a sexless marriage is craving that intimacy and acceptance.
- The same-sex-attracted person is looking for that intimacy and acceptance.

13. Bruce Marshall, *The World, the Flesh, and Father Smith* (Boston: Houghton Mifflin, 1945), 108.

In fact, female prostitutes say that not a few of their clients come looking, not for sex or a cheap release but only to be held tenderly and spoken to kindly, often like their mothers never did. It is a remarkable fact about humans. We all need what humans were made for and we seek it in all kinds of counterfeit places.

Most of these seekers are not "evil" because they seek to meet this need for intimacy in these various ways. They are seeking that which God has put within them, but have been told by the enemy that these other ways will satisfy them just as well as what God has for them. But of course they don't.

This truth should not make us angry or condemning toward others but compassionate and sad. Our anger should be properly pointed to the one who deceives and destroys.

This is true for us and for them. In fact, in a very real sense, there is no "us" and "them." We are all prodigal children.

Nonnegotiables for Evangelicals
toward Same-Sex-Attracted People

1. All people—including the same-sex-attracted and others of alternative sexual desires—are lovingly and individually created by God in His image and likeness.

2. Thus, Christianity uniquely affirms the equal dignity and value of all people and each must be encountered and treated accordingly.

3. Same-sex-attracted people, as with anyone, should not be singled out for special attention either negatively or positively, as there is nothing "worse" or "better" about them. They are people and as such, equal with all others.

4. It is the duty of the Christian to befriend the same-sex-attracted person, not necessarily toward any end, but simply to receive them as God's beloved, be their friend and learn to love them as people, as valuable individuals.

5. And like all friendships, the other person who we are befriending should generally be able to sense our love for and commitment to them as people. (However, as in any relationships, sometimes others simply cannot accept our friendship. There is nothing we can do about that.)

6. These friendships should be able to tolerate disagreements on sexual ethics and practice and still be friends. These differences should be shared with honesty, humility, and love, but not necessarily stated up front. Do this as the relationship naturally develops and matures, as trust between the friends is established.

7. The fundamental disease affecting all human beings is that our sin separates us eternally from God. No one is naturally immune to this.

8. Christianity—being established by and upon the person of Christ—is about the call and invitation to all people regarding their need for honest repentance, forgiveness, and redemption toward God and others through their journey toward relationship, obedience, and wholeness in Christ.

9. All people, in all places, have this need. And we all have the same hope of forgiveness in Christ's sacrificial death for each of us. It is the great equalizer.

10. These make all humans equal in standing and hope, create the same requirements for all human beings, and offer the same opportunity for a new life.

Toward Homosexuality

1. Scripture is clear from the first page that sexuality is a remarkably special creation and good gift of God, given with the first man and woman as they were commanded to enter its union from the beginning for the purpose

of love, union, and the creation of new life. God, as its Creator, takes great delight in our participation in it as well as our obedience to and respect for His design of it.

2. The relationship that God gives for sexual union is singularly within the protective confines of a faithful and self-giving communion of husband and wife.

3. There is no instance—explicit or implied—in the Old or New Testaments of any sexual union or behavior being blessed or ordained by God except between a faithfully married man and women.

4. Jesus unequivocally affirmed the creation-based truth of human sexuality when asked about the topic of marriage in Matthew 19 and Mark 10.

> Have you not read that he who created them from the beginning made them male and female, and said, "Therefore a man shall leave his mother and father and hold fast to his wife, and the two shall become one flesh? So they are no longer two but one flesh"?

5. No one, Christian or otherwise, has the right or power to rewrite God's directions, regardless of what that might be.

6. People are much more than their sexual desires and therefore to define one's self by these desires alone is to diminish one's full humanity.

7. Male and female, marriage and family are not so-called cultural constructs. An androgenized humanity, family, and culture are all culturally constructed and artificially forced upon a culture by ideological and political pressure.

8. It does not follow that same-sex attraction or identity is like either ethnicity or race. No sexual attraction is. While most who use this connection certainly don't mean anything unfair by it, it can be emotionally manipulative to suggest they are, as it can tend to paint one who doesn't agree with homosexuality as an equivalent to Southern Segregationists and all the ugliness that involved. And some mean exactly that. I have seen that very comparison and accusation used countless times toward me and others and it's simply a conversation stopper. One doesn't try to understand and become friends with a racist, do they? And in our conversations with our LGBT friends, it is not wrong to kindly ask them to consider how that must sound and feel from your point of view.

3

THE PROBLEM
OF FALSE CHOICES

Imagine this scenario. You're on the stand in court, testifying on behalf of your mother who's been arrested for robbing her local bank. Yes, your dear, sweet mom. You were with her that morning as she stopped by to deposit the monthly donations for the women's shelter where she volunteers three days a week. But there was an incident at the bank, which is why you are on the witness stand.

The prosecuting attorney is cross-examining you, and you're required to answer his questions in all honesty or you will be found in contempt of court or guilty of perjury. The fact that she's your mother cannot sway your answers to his questions. This is serious business. The prosecutor asks you, "Mrs. Franklin, isn't it true that on the morning of June 6, your mother entered the First Continental Bank on Robart Street, went to the counter and took, with her own hand, $2,800 of the bank's money from behind the teller's counter and put it right in her purse? And isn't it also true that she did this while every employee and customer in the bank was desperately frightened for their precious lives at gunpoint? Isn't this true, Mrs. Franklin?"

You start to answer his question honestly and directly: "What you say is technically true, but actually it was a bit different from that. You see ..." You are summarily interrupted and sharply commanded by this attorney to *answer the question*!! He repeats the questions and you try again, "Well, it's not that simple. You see ..."

The attorney, acting as if you are trying to hide the truth by kicking up all kinds of dust, responds by shouting, "Now, I'm only going to ask you one more time. Did your mother, or did she not, take that money from behind the counter while others feared for their lives? Yes or no? It's a simple question. Please, just answer!"

You look at the judge to see if you really do have to answer the questions. He informs you that you do and that you are under oath. You answer simply, with a remorseful look of "I am so sorry, Mother" in your eyes. You answer with a barely audible "Yes." The attorney, for the sake of courtroom dramatics, says, "I'm sorry, Mrs. Franklin. I couldn't hear you clearly. Could you state your answer one more time for the court, this time a little louder?"

You did what the court required, but while your answer was technically the truth, it was also false. How can that be?

Well, such things can happen when someone is trying to make *their* point and wants to make it more difficult for you to disagree with them. It's called a fallacy of the false choice. You know that your mother did take the money from behind the counter, and without the permission of the bank. As she did so, people in the bank were indeed screaming for their very lives as guns were drawn and pointed at the customers and employees. That much was absolutely true. But there is more that needs knowing.

Your mom was at the counter of the bank, transacting her deposit. One of the actual bank robbers was in line behind her. Frustrated at how long your mother was taking with her business—you know, she's getting up in years and her eyesight is not what it used to be—he stepped in, drew his gun, and demanded all the money in the vault. As the banker left his post to do as the gunman demanded, the robber instructed your mother to reach across the counter and take the large stacks of hundred-dollar bills in the banker's tray and stash those bills in her purse, which of course she did. He was going to take her with him as a hostage and shrewdly thought it safer if they left the bank with the money in her purse. She was doing just this as the police came in, drew their guns, and told everyone to freeze.

Of course, your mom always does what law enforcement says one must do. So she froze just where she was, putting the loot in her purse. Finding a shooter standing right next to her as she's doing this didn't look good for your mom because the robber insisted she was his accomplice, a perfect decoy. And thus, this was why she was on trial, albeit a trial that was going to clearly result in her exoneration, but not if the prosecution could help it.

As such, this attorney was not interested in the fuller story, the other critical details of the events that morning at the bank. He demanded a black-and-white, yes-or-no answer to his very simplistic and direct question. Sometimes—perhaps most often—the absolutist, black-and-white understanding of the facts has to be challenged in order to get to the real truth.

This is also true for numerous issues in today's public square. Many of their actual truths are found somewhere in the middle between the black-and-white extremes: All pro-lifers only care about babies while all pro-choicers support abortion at all costs; Democrats care for the poor while Republicans only care about rich people; country folks are not as sophisticated as city folk, etc. Many issues have angles to them that are often less simple than they first appear or are made out to be by their partisans.

This is true with many of the issues surrounding some of the LGBT movement's talking points and some of the Christian community's actions, attitudes, and language to those in that community. Too often, this issue unfortunately seems to be an exchange of ideas and accusations built only on stereotypical extremes and emotionalism, rather than rational thinking, genuine listening, and appreciation of the fundamental disagreements over things that are actually true to either side. It makes for good fireworks and twenty-four-hour cable show news clips, but it doesn't help us deal with the issues in any substantive and truly truthful way, which is essential for meaningful relationship.

Reality is usually a bit more complicated than we like to admit. This complexity makes things difficult to wade through. It's hard work, and most of us at times prefer the easy way of accepting the stereotype, what "everybody knows." In this chapter, we address some of the most prevalent false choices and try to honestly get at the important truths that lie somewhere between the extremes. We will deal with one of the biggest first.

Bigots vs. Perverts

No, this one is not a neighborhood softball match between the local white supremacists and the community's child pornographers. It marks the two extreme ways many on each side of this issue tend to understand and therefore paint their opponents.

Too many of the traditional-values folks have tended to see homosexuals as a horde of sex-crazed opportunists who go from bathhouse to bathhouse and cruise the public restrooms at the local parks, eager to score some anonymous action. Fewer, but still some, assume that most gays and lesbians are likely child molesters. But this stereotype certainly does not typify most same-sex-attracted people. Such assumptions and accusations are unfounded, unfair, and unkind. The majority of gay and lesbian people are simply trying to develop meaningful relationships the best they can—like the rest of us.

Now . . . it does no good to pretend that cruising and hooking up are *not* a significant part of the gay community and gay culture. Many in the gay community itself complain about this, especially the lesbians who don't understand why guys have to be so sexually adventurous and risk-taking.

And of course, the hetero community is not made up of choirboys (or choir girls) either.

On the other side, a widely held misperception—even by many evangelicals themselves—is that Christians who oppose same-sex marriage and same-sex parenting and such are motivated by bigotry and so-called homophobia. Major state and federal court decisions have said as much in support of their decisions, based purely on assumption. It has become a truism that those who oppose these things are haters, simply for the convictions they hold rather than any actual bigoted or hateful actions or words. Most cultural elites

> It has become a truism that those who oppose same-sex marriage are haters.

have uncritically accepted and contributed to this stereotyped script simply because they can imagine it being true based on Christians they have never met. Just like we can assume the child-molester charge about same-sex-attracted people we've never met.

Both of these ways of thinking are prejudice, judging someone simply because of what one assumes about them. And as if it needs saying, prejudice is wrong.

Clearly there have been those churches and individuals who act shamefully in the name of Christ toward individuals who are same-sex-attracted. One abominable instance is shown in a video on the Internet of a cute young boy standing before his congregation, singing a song with a chorus that explains, "Ain't no homos gonna make it to heaven" to the raucous applause of the congregation. Now I would trust that such a thing would horrify you as a Christian and would never happen at your church, and if it did, the folks who did it would be in a world of trouble with the church leadership and the congregation.

But in this instance, the pastors on the platform and the whole congregation were knee-slapping, hand-clapping, and laughing up a storm. Thankfully, incidences like these and the "God hates Fags" demonstrators (who have picketed Focus on the Family because they think we are too soft on this issue) have been strongly and publicly denounced by many in the Christian community who still strongly oppose the main-streaming of homosexuality.

Both sides on this issue have been guilty of uncivil and just plain mean behavior. But to be honest, as one who has paid very close attention to and participated in this issue for more than a decade, I am glad to say that there has been more calling out one's peers for correction and denunciation within the evangelical community than there has been within the LGBT community. That's just a fact that should be noted.

That is not to say that we are better, for we have a higher standard as Christians regarding loving behavior toward those we disagree with. And we have some serious things to answer for and we should be willing to do so. But to assume—as so many do—that we essentially have one side of haters and abusers and one side of tolerance-embracing victims in this issue is simplistic and untrue. And any friendship that operates under this assumption rests on a faulty base. It has been a pretty ugly discussion all the way around so far with no one earning any gold star for their behavior. That is what we hope to help change with this book.

We all have plenty of opportunity to do better and we must, but it can't just be based on happy-talk. It must be genuine, person-to-person, without ignoring the real issues that divide us. Grace *and* truth. The next false choice is related to this one.

Friend or Enemy? Pick One

Equally disturbing is the idea that if you want to be my friend, you must agree with me. If you don't agree with me, then you've chosen to be my enemy: a dramatic problem of false choices.

A professor who teaches anthropology at a Christian college on the East Coast wrote a provocative and intelligent book on the current public discussion on gender and sexual identity.[1] In the introduction, she tells an

---

1. Jenell Williams Paris, *The End of Sexual Identity* (Downers Grove, IL: InterVarsity, 2011).

interesting story from her time in graduate school where she had become friends with a bisexual woman who was an atheist. Our professor-to-be was a good evangelical girl and her new friend announced one day, "I want to take you to a gay bar and see if you can handle it." She accepted the invitation, not so much because she wanted to go to a gay bar, but as an anthropologist, she was interested in experiencing and learning about new subcultures. As well, she wanted to demonstrate to her new friend that she was willing to do something for her that took a bit of courage and was outside her box. She was asked if she had ever been to a gay bar. Of course she said no but kept it to herself that she had *never* been to *any* kind of bar!

So she went, hung with her friend's regular crew for the evening and learned some things her quiet evangelical upbringing and conviction had never exposed her to. While there, her friend asked her, "So, now that you are on my turf, let me ask you this: Does Christianity really condemn homosexuality?"

Of course she blushed with embarrassment and discomfort at such a blunt question in such a setting, but she didn't shy from the question. As she explained her response in the book, she really did a remarkable job of grace and truth. She was very kind in explaining what the Bible has historically taught on sexuality—

> "I stood up for my faith, so why did I feel my faith had let me down?"

that it is a gift from God and is only to be shared between a husband and wife. She spoke about what she was for, what she believed in the positive, and not so much of what she was against. Smart road to take. She concluded by saying, "I don't have the right to revise centuries of Christian teaching." Her friend, in front of the group, told her strongly and without hesitation, "Well, then I can't be friends with a homophobe." Wow.

The author says she felt bad about her answer and what it did to hurt her friend. She explained, upon reflection, that it seems as if "homosexuality is a sin" is the only message that Christians have for same-sex-attracted people and being a faithful Christian requires repeating that over and over again to all who will listen. She explained, "My friend felt judged by my response to her at the bar, and though I spoke in a measured (maybe even hesitant) tone, my words sounded judgmental to me too. I stood up for my faith, so why did I feel like my faith had let me down?"[2]

What would you have done in such a situation? How would you have acted and responded in...

- Establishing such a friendship in the first place?
- Taking her up on her invitation to join her and her friends at the bar?
- Answering her question?
- Her friend's response to her question?
- Your own feelings to her response?

These are important questions and ones that more of us should have to face as we discern how we can step out of the safe, neat Christian boxes we have protectively constructed for ourselves. As one who is in similar situations quite often, I was troubled by our professor's reflections and feelings about the incident when I read it. Let me explain.

First, of course her willingness and effort to be this woman's friend was a great and important thing to do. It took great courage to go to the bar that evening. It was a strong sign of willingness for friendship. (Although one must give such an option much prayer, being mindful whether you have the maturity to handle such a thing in a healthy way.[3])

---

2. Jenell Williams Paris, 8.
3. In 1 Corinthians 5:9, Paul clearly says that Christians should not associate with sexually immoral people, so why would I encourage believers in situations like this to do precisely that? Because of what Paul says next in verse 10. He explains he is not speaking of the immoral people in the world, for "then you would need to go out of the world." He says we should not "associate with anyone who bears the name of brother" [or sister] if they live without remorse in their immorality of various types, not just sexual (v. 11).

I thought she did a wonderful job, honest yet gracious, of answering the question put to her.

What really troubled me was the last two parts of the incident. Let me start with the last part. The professor-to-be was asked a question—uncomfortably, even rudely, put on the spot in a place that was strange to her—and she answered that question as honestly as she could. She answered it factually, directly, but with no unnecessary sermonizing or judgmentalism.

It was the woman who asked the question and she got a truthful and kind answer. This reminds me of a marvelous line in the last scene of the movie *Pulp Fiction*. Vincent (actor John Travolta) and Jules (Samuel L. Jackson) are at breakfast at a Denny's-type restaurant talking about some big "meaning-of-life" questions. Jules is taking it much more seriously than Vincent, and Vincent says he just wants to end the conversation and eat his bacon. Jules matter-of-factly looks Vincent squarely in the eyes and tells him, "If you find my answers frightening, Vincent, you should cease asking scary questions." That is exactly the advice the professor's friend should have taken. Don't ask questions if you might not like the answer and certainly don't condemn the person for answering it kindly and honestly.

It would have been one thing if the author had said to the crew in the bar that night all on her own, "While I have you all together, can I tell you guys what Christianity thinks of homosexuality?" Wrong place, wrong time. But the friend was clearly ill-mannered to put her new friend on the spot ("since we're on my turf"), when good manners would have called for just spending time together and getting to know one another, which is what our professor was set on doing.

Not only that, but the author's friend told her they could no longer be friends and called her an ugly name, while totally missing the fact that a real-life homophobe is not likely to actually accept an invitation to a gay bar. It was the Christian woman who was willing to take the chance and step out and into a part of her new friend's world. Her friend couldn't or wouldn't see that this Christian student was the first one to make a real effort at friendship that had actually cost her something. If someone was insensitive here, it certainly wasn't the Christian and she shouldn't have felt bad.

"Either accept all of me, even my personal convictions, or we can't be friends." No mature relationship works so conditionally, does it? On what other topic of disagreement do we establish such a criteria for friendship? Nobody should feel bad about being put in that position and refusing to be held hostage by it, regardless of which side of an issue you are on. Any Christian who demands that of an unbeliever is clearly and drastically wrong and rude.

A very good rule of thumb is to ask three questions in such relationships:

1. Does this person know that I care for them? (Not, *do* I, but do they *know* it themselves—from my actions, my commitment to and friendship with them, and my words.)
2. Do they also know why I disagree with them and they with me? (Do they know my convictions and why I hold them? Do I know theirs? Have we talked about this in an honest and civil way?)
3. Can we maintain an honest, caring, self-giving relationship based on these realities?

If you cannot answer yes to each of these questions—and it typically and properly takes months to establish each of these—then it is most likely you are skimping on either grace or truth, and both of them are necessary for an authentic, meaningful friendship, regardless of who the friendship includes.

Homosexuals Have No Place in the Church?

When we arrived at the Q&A part of a debate on sexual ethics at Fresno State University a number of years ago, a young man stood and asked me a direct question, "What would your church do with a guy like me if I showed up one Sunday morning?" My first response was to play by the rules set by most university settings and properly so. I asked, "As it would be wrong of me to make any assumptions about you, let me ask, what kind of guy are you?" I was sincere and it was on him to explain what it was he was actually talking about. His answer, "a queer." The audience laughed with him, assuming I was in a tough spot now. Some may have thought I'd be forced to say, "Well I'd grab you by the scruff of the neck and send you airborne through the closest window, because we don't like your type."

Here is what I was happy to tell him:

"We would be most happy and honored to have 'someone like you' come to our church. We would welcome you, give you a sincere and hearty hug, as we do everyone, and invite you to sit anywhere you wanted. We would even find someone to sit with you so you wouldn't be alone. So that you would feel welcomed and not because we think you would scribble naughty words and dirty pictures in the hymnals."

And I can tend to be an optimist, but I trust that most other evangelical churches would do pretty much the same thing. At least I hope they would. And those that wouldn't need to check their theology and where they stand on the whole "who are the sinners?" question.

I went on to address the bigger question that I sensed was behind his question: "What would your church do with someone like me who you see as a sinner? Could you handle it?"

Of course, the answer is that every church could (and perhaps should) have a sign over their doors that announces "Non-sinners need not apply," for sinners are the only people the church knows how to deal with. And it does every Sunday when we are there, *because* we are there. Sinners are the only people our Savior knows how to deal with.

And here, I'm gonna call author's privilege and assert that no good Christian should ever utter the phrase "You don't clean your car before you go to a car wash, do you?" regarding this truth. Why? Churches aren't car washes and people aren't cars. It's not clever, just corny. Now back to where we were.

All sinners should expect a warm and welcoming reception to any Christ-honoring church. And no sinner— liars, cheats, gossipers, the proud and arrogant, backstabbers, and all who deal with sexual sin, which includes most all of us—can expect a pass on their sin. The call to repentance that both John the Baptist and Jesus proclaimed applies to all. And while that repentance is a part of the process of discipleship as a Christian, it is not a requirement for *starting* to come to church, is it? I certainly wouldn't have been able to start attending church if this was the case, and I trust you wouldn't have either.

> "Well pray tell, just what *does* a Christian look like?"

But what about the sinner who has been attending awhile, come to call Christ their Lord, and it doesn't look like they are cleaning up their junk? Pastor Chuck Smith, a pastor in Southern California who had a huge impact on the Jesus Movement and beyond, remembered how he was constantly challenged by his congregation when the barefoot, long-haired, smelly, weird-talking, dope-smoking hippies actually started coming to their church. Chuck gave the regular attendees an ultimatum. "If they have to go, I have to go!"

Put in a corner, they then asked, "Well, when are they going to start looking like Christians?"

Pastor Chuck would put his hand on their shoulder and gently ask, "Well pray tell, just what *does* a Christian look like?" And then he would explain, "How 'bout we trust the Holy Spirit to convict them of what He wants to convict them of. In the meantime we'll do our best to faithfully teach the Word and love them the best we can."

That answer always impressed me as remarkably wise, patient, and confident in the working of the Holy Spirit. And the same holds today for all the "strange people" we hope will attend our churches.

Do homosexuals belong in the church? Of course they do. It's really the best place they do belong, as do all of us. It should be the primary place where they should really be loved unconditionally, served by others, and encouraged to serve others. In a way, it is really this simple for all churches:

1. Welcome all who want to come.
2. Faithfully and lovingly teach the whole Word of God without compromise.
3. Let the Holy Spirit do His work and you try to cooperate with His leading.

But sometimes it gets more complicated than that. A pastor of a very strong and faithful Bible-teaching (and living) church in Chicago's Andersonville neighborhood, on the edge of a leading gay community, has a number of gay and lesbian individuals and couples who come to his church regularly. This pastor and his congregation are trying to do the above three things as best they can where they are. A few gay and lesbian individuals and couples have asked if they can get involved doing various jobs during services: ushering, handing out bulletins, making sure kids don't take more donuts than they should, stacking chairs, nursery duty, etc. First rule of pastoring: "Don't refuse volunteer help!"

Real-Life Questions Churches Should Grapple With

But what about *these* folks? What can they do, and is there anything they should not do? These are big real-life questions that more churches should grapple with. Their church elders had to address these questions prayerfully and wisely in light of their biblical conviction and mission in the community.

I will let Bill Shereos, a new friend and the senior pastor of this church, explain some of these struggles:

"Many who visit our Sunday service of worship reflect our community's demographic. This involves people of various ages, races, classes, religion, and sexual orientation. So how do we live out genuine Christian community in this context? It is here we experience tension and challenge and where difficult questions arise, such as:

- How do we love and receive all people while holding to a biblical standard, including a traditional understanding of the biblical sexual ethic?
- How do we allow people to be 'in process' yet at the same time challenge them toward maturity in Christ?
- How do we make disciples beginning with where people are rather than where we'd like them to be?

"Our church claims no expertise in ministering to our LGBT neighbors. In fact, we have had only small successes and often stumble as we seek to follow God's Holy Spirit. We have not targeted our LGBT neighbors in our outreach efforts but we've made a very conscious decision to invite and welcome all of our neighbors regardless of color, economic class, or sexual orientation. As a result, we've encountered 'new' situations I could have never anticipated when I began ministry decades ago. It's both exciting and challenging."

The church found itself needing to rethink its volunteer policy when a gay couple volunteered to help in the church nursery, having adopted children of their own. Pastor Shereos recalls how the church honored its existing policy (see the account on the next page). He recommends that "each church ... determine where appropriate lines need to be drawn in their particular situation, being sure not to over- , but not underreact either. We are to walk through our lives with others with grace and truth. We are thankful that God has entrusted us with challenges like this." He describes how his church responded when a gay couple in the community and their adopted children became regular attendees at the church.

> This required us to rethink our volunteer policy. We have a practice that parents who have children in our nursery are asked to be volunteers in the nursery. As this new family began attending and of course, bringing their young children to our nursery, some in our congregation pushed back against this policy, saying, "Would we be endorsing the gay lifestyle if we allowed them to volunteer?"
>
> The church leadership needed to meet to think and pray through how we should proceed. Our elders decided that we would require of this couple what we do of all others, no more, no less.
>
> We would require the same expectations and background check we require for every children's ministry volunteer. Our elders also affirmed that regular attendees who do not follow our church's sexuality policy would be allowed to volunteer in "serving ministries" but not "teaching or discipling ministries." This also challenged us to consider that there may be other volunteers in our nursery who violate our church's sexuality policy in various ways. We began asking ourselves what we are doing to help all our church attendees in the process of following Jesus more closely.
>
> While we require our members to seek a biblical standard in their sexual ethic, we realize that not all who attend our Sunday service of worship are fully committed to Jesus and live according to biblical standards. Yet if our local assembly is going to be a place where people are learning about Jesus and learning to follow Him, of course there will be some who are

still in the early stages of considering His lordship. And this can make ministry messy, in a good way, for all the new folks who come to our church and seek a life as a Christian.

This situation occurred several years ago and put us on alert that we must always be willing to face new challenges as we consider how we make disciples of those God brings to our door. It also helped us affirm that while we need to hold members to a biblical sexual ethic, we do not want to exclude people who are in a seeking mode from our services of worship. This event was also helpful in helping us intentionally include our LGBT neighbors in ministries such as our Community Care Clinic. We've found many members of the LGBT community to be especially caring and compassionate toward the poor. As some have served in such ministries, they have experienced Christian community and have decided to connect with our congregation more closely, even though they may not completely agree with all of our policies regarding sexuality. That's exciting for a pastor and his congregation to see.

This is certainly not the only way or perhaps even the best way to handle people who don't agree with a church's sexual ethic. Yet perhaps it may help you to think through your own understanding of Christian ministry in a secular context.[4]

Who Are You to Tell Me I'm Wrong?

I get this question nearly every time I speak on this issue at a secular campus. It usually comes with a bit of an edge to it and is usually followed by robust applause from the audience. The question is similar to the

---

4. From personal communication with Pastor Bill Shereos, senior pastor of First Free, an Evangelical Free church in Chicago.

dilemma faced by the anthropology grad student we just met. This is a problem of a false choice, assuming that to hold a position contrary to someone else and explain what that position is, is bad form. There's a better way to say such things, for we unfortunately see much too much crass rudeness in such situations today. And its source is often spiritual pride. But the key is to try to present your views, regardless of the issue, with insight, much study, forthrightness, and a genuinely humble and gracious manner behind it. I can often fail at the "humble" and "gracious" parts, but such a goal is a nonnegotiable. Here's how I answer this question:

After the applause for the question dies down, I smile just a bit, wait a few seconds to collect myself, and then answer by making two obvious points.

One, I explain that I was invited here tonight by the group sponsoring the event for the very purpose of explaining to you what it is I believe, because of what I believe. "And I certainly don't want to let them down" often gesturing to the person from the organization who introduced the speakers and the evening. That breaks the ice for all of us. I add, "And I assume you're telling me I'm wrong for telling you you're wrong. See any inconsistency there?"

I then pull out a little piece of paper from my wallet and ask them if they know what it might be. Of course they don't, it's too small. "It's my voter registration card," I say, and then I explain that contrary to popular opinion,

"We in the religious right [I use that descriptor in a self-deprecating way] don't get three votes to everyone else's one vote. We get one vote. And I use this card to vote my convictions. You have a card—if you're registered to vote, and you should be—that allows you to vote your convictions as well. And the answer to this from any of our particular political perspectives is not to keep people from voting that have an opposing view, but to encourage those who agree with us to vote. This is the fuel that a vibrant democracy runs on and it is enriched by more and diverse participation, not less. And that is why you should get involved as well." I also explain that our nation's value of freedom of speech gives me one voice. Not two, not six. Just one. And I try to use mine the best way I know how, and you should do the same thing. "So, to answer your question," I conclude, "that is why any of us have the right to tell anyone else they are wrong."

And then the crowd responds, which is about the only time I ever get any applause. Curiously, I have held up the more truly liberal ethic of diversity and freedom of speech and expression. My questioner was actually holding up, unwittingly, the suppression of that speech. My answer helped the crowd understand that.

But this is most important. Expressing an opinion that is contrary to someone else's is obviously saying the person is wrong, but this is the logical outcome of stating any opinion. "I think we can cross the street now." "No, we can't yet. The little walking-man sign hasn't turned white yet." Someone just told someone else they were wrong. It's unavoidable in a world where there are objective facts and personal beliefs about those facts. All of us, sooner or later, are on the receiving end of "You're wrong!" As long as one holds any opinion or conviction, it is unavoidable.

> Peace is the virtuous manner in which we engage others in the face of disagreement.

But the big question is how we communicate this disagreement, for we should strive to disagree without being disagreeable. It is true. We can do it with great passion and conviction, but as much as possible we should always do so with civility and consideration to the person we are disagreeing with. Remember what Paul exhorted us to do in Romans 12:18: "If possible, so far as it depends on you, live peaceably with all."

As much as it is possible, and sometimes it is not, live at peace with others. Peace is not always agreement or even the absence of disagreement. It is the virtuous manner in which we engage others in the face of disagreement.

Born This Way or Choice?

This is probably one of the most widely held and asserted false choices in this issue: "We were born this way." Lady Gaga is not the only one who tells us that gay, lesbian, bisexual, and transgendered folks are "born this way." On the other side, many religious conservative and general traditionalists say they choose to be this way.

Dr. James Dobson, my boss for many years at Focus on the Family, appeared on *Larry King Live* one evening, taking Mr. King's questions in rapid-fire succession. One of them was "Is homosexuality genetic or a choice?" Dr. Dobson answered the question, recognizing it as a false choice, by saying "Neither." At that moment, Mr. King said, "We'll be right back with more questions for Dr. James Dobson" and then went to his scheduled commercial break. As they came back, King dove right into more questions. Dr. Dobson never got to fill out the rest of his answer, explaining why it was neither a matter of choice or nature.

In the following days we got thousands of phone calls and pieces of mail wondering why Dr. Dobson ducked the question. They assumed it was either one or the other, black-or-white, yes or no, and Doc just wanted to avoid the controversy. As we always do at Focus, we answered each inquiry personally and fully. The real answer to this question, not surprisingly, is more complicated than these two choices. So . . . what's the right answer?

The actual answer to this question has significant implications. There has been a very concerted effort over the last thirty years to find the so-called gay gene, which essentially means some genetic cause behind same-sex attraction proving the "born-that-way" perspective. The famously liberal Bishop John Spong of the Episcopal Church explained the implications of the success in finding such a "natural" reason in the late 1990s: "When homosexual orientation is revealed by the science of the brain and neurochemical processes to be a normal part of the sexual spectrum of human life, a given and not a chosen way of life, then it becomes inhuman to use a person's sexual orientation as the basis for continuing prejudice."[5]

The political and rhetorical implications of this are clear and have worked themselves out today: If homosexuality is natural, simply what people are genetically, then anything that is not affirming to homosexuality is "inhumane" and not to affirm it is "prejudice." This is clearly a very dramatic politicization of a question that largely resides in the domain of science.

First, in getting at the truth between the two extremes, we must recognize, as we noted earlier, that the public debate often mashes up the Ls, the Gs, the Bs, and the Ts in LGBT as if these four letters—much less the long chain regularly being added to it—speak of one or even similar things. If it does, it's only of a sociopolitical identity and not so much a practical or sexual identity, as these are all very different psychosexual expressions in themselves as evidenced by the fact that each letter specifies something unique from the others, right? As such, there is no such thing as an "LGBT person" or an "LGBT identity" per se. It signifies a group identity. And quite often, as we also saw, they can tend to be at odds with one another ideologically, politically, and socially from time to time, in very significant ways. So to say that if there is a genetic indicator for male same-sex attraction doesn't mean that this also necessarily true for being bisexual or transgendered, or even for lesbianism. They are each different things.

For instance, on the same-sex attraction side of things, the nature of male same-sex attraction has important and marked differences from female same-sex attraction. The Gs seem to be much more "fixed" or constant in the objects of their sexual desire than the Ls, who are generally observed to be more flexible (demonstrating a greater plasticity, as

---

5. John Spong, *Why Christianity Must Change or Die: A Bishop Speaks to Believers in Exile* (San Francisco: HarperSanFrancisco, 1998), 161.

the specialists call it) and are more culturally/socially influenced.[6] So, in exploring this question, we must recognize that these various sexual desires or orientations are all quite different from each other in important ways.

"It's a Choice"

Let's start with the "choice" side of the question, as it's an easier one to deal with. Some who believe homosexuality is a choice see it working something like this. One drives down the road of life, developing in physical, emotional, and sexual maturity as a human being. They are starting to become aware of their sexual desires and interests and they see a fork in the road. One way is marked "heterosexuality" and the other marked "homosexuality." They see a lot of people taking one of the paths, but they decide the other road, the one less traveled, might be interesting. So they choose that path. They decide that is who and what they want to be.

Simple. Except that it's not.[7]

The less naïve view suspects that while it's not as simple as the fork-in-the-road choice, they do assume that gay and lesbian individuals "choose" to follow any confusing feelings of same-sex attraction they might have, just as a young boy with gender identity disorder (GID) might feel he is more comfortable as a girl and then commits to being what he senses he really is. This second view allows for a sense of

---

6. Just two journal articles as examples from this notable body of literature are: Roy F. Baumeister, "Gender Difference in Erotic Plasticity: The Female Sex Drive as Socially Flexible and Responsive," *Psychological Bulletin* 126 (2000): 347–74; Lisa M. Diamond, "The Evolution of Plasticity in Female-Female Desire," *Journal of Psychology & Human Sexuality* 18 (2007): 245–74.

7. Among lesbians, there are more than a few who definitively decide that this is the way they are going to be, out of preference, as a social statement or because of the hurt they have experienced by men. Men are nearly never likely to "choose" same-sex sexual intimacy as something they want to explore without having felt some strong internal pull in that direction.

"this-is-the-way-I-am" but maintaining that it is finally a choice to actively follow and act on those senses of oneself.

There is some complex truth to this side of things, but becoming same-sex-attracted is not a "choice" as we typically think of it. Many same-sex-attracted males will ask you, "If it's a choice, why would I have chosen such a difficult life?" They have a point.

"One Is Born That Way"

This view essentially holds that being same-sex-attracted is a physiological matter. It is simply what one is born with, what they are born *as*. It is what one *is*. It contends that being a homosexual is a product of genetics, hormones, or the kind of brain one is born with. It asserts that nature creates all kinds of different people: white people, short people, yellow people, hairy people, skinny people, brown people, fast people, introverted people, curly haired people, and homosexual or bisexual people. This is largely an unquestioned assumption today. Except it is not a truth. At least there is no reliable science that has shown it to be true. And this is simply not in dispute among those on either side who have carefully studied this issue.

There has been no shortage of vigorous, sophisticated research by skilled and highly motivated researchers looking for a biological or genetic source of same-sex attraction for the last twenty to thirty years. And given this robust effort, studying it from many different angles, there is no scientific consensus at all on whether either male-male or female-female sexual attraction is rooted solely or even primarily in genetic, hormonal, or neural development. Not even close. And there don't seem to be any corners to search, couches to look under, or dressers to check behind in the human physiology where such a cause might be hiding. They've searched everywhere, and nothing has come up.

Also, each of the numerous studies conducted have had significant methodological problems that bring doubt to their conclusions. And the findings have yet to be replicated in any subsequent studies, a necessary standard of scientific validity. Dr. Richard Horton, the longtime editor-in-chief of the prestigious British medical journal *The Lancet*, carefully addressed the troubles with this body of research and the effort to find the "gay gene" in a lengthy review of some new academic books on the subject in the *New York Review of Books*. There he explained:

> The search for a single dominant gene . . . that would influence a behavioral variant is likely to be fruitless. Many different genes, together with many different environmental [or experiential] factors, will interact in unpredictable ways to guide behavioral preferences. The quest for a teleological explanation to identify a reason for the existence of a "gay gene" becomes pointless when one understands that there is not now, and never was, a single and final reason for being gay or straight, or having any other identity along the continuum of sexual preference.[8]

Later in the *Review of Books* article, Dr. Horton adds: "Researchers ignore the central issue in the debate over nature and nurture. The question is: How do genes get you from a biochemical program that instructs cells to make proteins to an unpredictable interplay of behavioral impulses—fantasy, courtship, arousal, sexual selection—that constitutes 'sexuality'? The question remains unresolved."

Horton is saying that this matter is far too complicated a human question to be explained by either of these extremes or by any explanation today that claims to capture the true nature of how same-sex attraction develops. This is exactly what Dr. Dobson was getting at with Larry King. We just don't and perhaps can't know. The American Psychiatric

---

8. Richard Horton, "Is Homosexuality Inherited?" *New York Review of Books*, July 1995. (Even though this article is from 1995, no findings since then have changed or challenged Horton's conclusion.)

Association, in commenting on the nature and development of sexual orientation, currently explains:

> There is no consensus among scientists about the exact reasons that an individual develops a heterosexual, bisexual, gay or lesbian orientation. Although much research has examined the possible genetic, hormonal, developmental, social and cultural influences on sexual orientation, no findings have emerged that permit scientists to conclude that sexual orientation is determined by any particular factor or factors. Many think that nature and nurture both play complex roles; most people experience little or no sense of choice about their sexual orientation.[9]

The American Academy of Pediatrics, in addressing the issue of same-sex attraction and adolescent patients, informs its doctors: "A variety of theories about the influences on sexual orientation have been proposed. Sexual orientation probably is not determined by any one factor but by a combination of genetic, hormonal, and environmental influences."[10]

And Camille Paglia, a noted author, professor, lesbian, gender theorist and dissident feminist who certainly doesn't follow anyone's cues in her thoughts and opinions, comes to the point on this topic bluntly: "No one is 'born gay.' The idea is ridiculous, but it is symptomatic of our overpoliticized climate that such assertions are given instant credence by gay activists and their media partisans. I think what gay men are remembering is that they were born *different*."[11]

Professor Paglia's last line is very insightful and touches on something

---

9. American Psychological Association, "Answers to Your Questions: For a Better Understanding of Sexual Orientation and Homosexuality" (Washington, DC: APA, 2008).

10. Barbara L. Frankowski, "Sexual Orientation and Adolescents," *Pediatrics*, 113 (2004): 1827–32.

11. Camille Paglia, *Vamps & Tramps: New Essays* (New York: Vintage Books, 1994), 72.

big. Many will say, "I never chose to be gay. I've just always been this way." Always seeming to be a certain way is very different than "I was born this way." I have always been moderately depressed and from time to time wished I could just not exist anymore. Curiously, I have felt this way ever since I can remember and know that I had these feelings when I was very young. And they have been quite substantial. But I wouldn't say that this is the way "I am" or that I was "born that way." But this certainly is and has been "how" I am, going on inside of me all along—there was never an age where I remember not being this way—and its development and existence within me is the result of a number of curious factors from psychological developments, home and parenting environments, chemical deficiencies, and my general views of my own life and self-worth.

We are complicated beings, especially when it comes to our sexuality. And anyone who tries to come up with a simple explanation is not appreciating how sophisticatedly and complexly God's design of the human being is, just as all the rest of His creation.

So What Causes It, and Why Does It Matter?

Bottom line, no one knows what determines one's sexual orientation, or even what sexual attractions denote an orientation and which do not. Is nonmonogamy an orientation? Nonmonogamists sometimes claim it is. Polyamorists say their desire for "many lovers"—what the word means and denotes—is their orientation. What about pedophilia, necrophilia, or hypersexuality?

Within the sciences, what qualifies one sexual desire as an orientation and another as not? There is no precise and agreed-upon answer. We only have ideas and opinions so far, but it is not from want of trying to find such a reason. But as we have seen in just a few examples, the consensus among mainstream researchers and scholars is that variations from heterosexuality seem to come from some unknown mix of both nature and nurture; physiological and developmental/experiential sources. It remains a mystery.

Simply put, human sexuality is a very complex and remarkable phenomenon that cannot easily be explained or understood.

So—why does this "born-this-way/choice" question matter to the question of how we love our LGBT neighbor? It's indeed an important question and here is the answer: because it affects how we see and understand the same-sex-attracted person, and therefore how we will tend to treat him or her. Let me explain.

The first reason is its general importance. The "this-or-that" way we tend to divide out this question of origin minimizes and simplifies the nature of the struggles, questions, and resolve that goes on inside the same-sex-attracted person, when and how they "come out," and how they mix in the larger society. To adhere to either a false choice or simplistic explanation is similar to someone saying, "I know exactly why people become Christians. Because they are afraid of going to hell and need a crutch to get through life." Imagine an unbeliever developing a relationship with you, believing this and therefore thinking they understand you and your commitment to your faith. There might be some truth to it, but it is very narrow and simplistic. We don't want to and can't be "that guy" in our growing relationships with our LGBT friends.

Now, some might be this way not because it is inherent in their personality and character whether gay, straight, or ambidextrous. As a friend's little boy told his parents, "Sometimes I like to be grumpy!" In short, signing up for the "it's a choice" school of thought can tend to make us unfeeling and more judgmental.

If nature simply determines that one will be same-sex-attracted, then we cannot and should not be against what someone just naturally is, right? And of course, we hear this often in the debate today: "Being gay, lesbian, and otherwise is just who someone is, just like being Asian, black, a man, or a woman . . ." Therefore, related to our faith, it is then God who makes one gay or lesbian, just like He makes one Caucasian, Native American, or Inuit. And whose place is it to deny or disapprove of what God created? And as Spong said, any lack of total acceptance, not just for the person but for their desires, is, to use his word, "prejudice."

> The result of being healed of any sin is holiness.

Therefore, pitching one's tent in the "born-this-way" camp compels us to accept homosexuality and homosexual behavior uncritically and as a mere variation of how one can be human. It can push us into the unfounded demand for full and uncritical acceptance.

But all kinds of things show up within us—both through some hereditary or genetic factor and/or our life experiences and environmental influences—that can be good and praiseworthy (physical strength or IQ), unfortunate and unnatural (conjoined twins or ambiguous genitalia), as well as unhealthy and best kept at bay in our lives (depression, alcoholism, heart disease), as hard as that might be. Unless we understand and appreciate this issue with the complexity it requires, we cannot really understand and appreciate the person who deals with it.

The born-that-way/choice narratives are simplistic and false choices, and we should not reduce the issue to those narratives.

Homosexuals Must Be Healed to Be Good Christians

Many in the church believe that if someone with same-sex attraction comes to accept Christ and puts themselves under His lordship as a Christian, they should be healed of their homosexuality. They assume the two cannot exist together. (We will address an important variant of this next.) But that would assume that the cure for homosexuality is heterosexuality. It is not. The result of being healed of any sin—yours, mine, others'—is holiness. There are many in the church today who have been healed of same-sex attraction and do not struggle with it anymore. There are those who have been delivered from it, yet still struggle from time to time—just as those who struggle with the sins of gossiping, lying, lusting, drug abuse, etc.

But there are also those who have never been healed or delivered. Like Paul, with his "thorn in the flesh,"[12] many just have to learn to live with it, seeking to be obedient day in and day out in the midst of it like most of us do with our issues. This brings us to a related false choice.

Same-Sex Attraction and Obedience to Christ Don't Mix

So what of the same-sex-attracted person who prays, works, goes to counseling for years and years, and never is freed of this desire? Or the Christian who makes no effort at all to be freed from that same desire? Is it possible for them to live an obedient and God-honoring life in accordance with the Scriptures and historic teaching of Christ's church and still have same-sex attraction?

The simple answer is, of course!

As we explored earlier, there is nothing wrong with wrong desires and temptations, per se. We all deal with them as a result of original sin. The Bible says that Christ was tempted in all the ways that we are but did not sin (Hebrews 4:15). What does this tell us? There is temptation and desire *here*. And there is sin *there*. The two are not the same.

Sin is giving in to a desire or temptation and participating in it. Obedience is properly resisting and fleeing the temptation or wrong desire. I sense that I want to lie to avoid getting into trouble or being embarrassed. What am I going to do with that temptation? I can give in and lie or resist it and tell the truth, whatever the cost. The temptation or desire is not the sin. Acting on it is. This is what Christ did, tempted but obedient. He can sympathize with our struggles because as a man, He

---

12. 2 Corinthians 12:7.

experienced them. This is a wonderfully hopeful truth in Christianity.

There are untold thousands of faithful and beautiful saints in so many churches across the world who are same-sex-attracted, struggling with those temptations, but have made a choice to live celibately because that is what God calls all people to when they have not entered into His plan for marriage. They know, like all of us should, that we don't have a right or the power to edit God's Book or His desires for us. He's the boss. Sin is serious business and God doesn't give us a pass because it's hard. But He does give us His Holy Spirit who abides with us, helps us, leads us into all truth, and comforts us in our struggles.

So yes, there are wonderful believers all around in our churches who are living as faithful disciples—and none do it perfectly—while also living with same-sex attraction. But they do so by bringing that desire in line with what God has commanded us regarding our sexuality. That is what a growing, faithful, vibrant disciple of Jesus seeks to do. And same-sex-attracted people do and can live this way with great joy and peace, just as unmarried heterosexuals should and do. And we should encourage all of them in this difficult walk and stand beside them as they live with such attraction in this very real and trying discipleship.

If You Love Me, You'll Accept Me as I Am

Although very similar to the "Agree with me or be a bigot" false choice, this is a tad different. It doesn't so much make an accusation against someone—"you bigoted hater!"—but simply asks that you accept them uncritically. What could possibly be wrong with that?

This attitude pits one's demand of your full acceptance of their sexuality against whatever love you might have for them. One might not mean this to be manipulative, but it actually is. Very good friends who really love one another have strong opinions about what the other does and doesn't do, and they remain friends in light of it.

Suppose a woman tells her best friend that she is thinking of having an affair with a man from work. You know her marriage has not been going well, and that her husband has not been attentive to your friend. And you know this man she is considering entering the affair with to be a relatively nice man. But you know what such a relationship would do to her, her husband, the other man's wife, and their children in the long run. So you tell her she's wrong and even selfish to even consider such a thing. She doesn't appreciate your advice, sees it as judgmental and says, "If you loved me, you would see how right this is for me."

Who of us would think what you did was mean? That all you need to do is loosen up and support your friend in what she wants to do? Who are you to judge? They're both adults, after all. No, we easily understand that disagreement and saying so is sometimes the only loving thing to do. For your friend to demand full agreement as a condition of a relationship is simply unreasonable. In fact, it is not too different from the child who is told he cannot have candy before dinner and responds: "Well, you hate me!" believing that this will force your hand. Good parents don't fall for it, and neither do good friends.

And we should be absolutely open to the same kinds of disagreement and challenges from our gay and lesbian friends regarding our lives. We cannot and should not expect them to accept our values or views of Scripture and the Christian life, if they don't. They very well might think we are delusional for truly believing that God could become man and raise Himself from the grave. They might even be hostile about it. Now we can talk to them about it, explain ourselves, try to persuade them but they have the right to their own thoughts on such subjects, don't they? Again, it is wrong for anyone to hinge the continuation of one's relationship on whether or not they agree or disagree with you on important things.

The Truth, Spoken in Love

What we need to do is be able to spot these false choices for what they are, in others and in ourselves, so they don't create artificial boundaries around what could be a very meaningful and important relationship. Any relationship that tolerates the existence of falsehood or the absence of truth is not an honest, authentic relationship. It is artificially constructed and maintained. While no relationship can withstand all truth all the time—"Do you know what else I think you did wrong today?"—it cannot withstand a constant avoidance of truth either. Healthy relationships find a proper balance.

And it is important to appreciate that the truth of matters often lies somewhere in the middle ground between extremes. And our relationships will become stronger when we seek to live gracefully in the truth, rather than in extreme and unfounded assumptions about each other based on the key talking points in the current public debate.

When truth is needed, it is spoken in humility and love. And that makes the relationship and the people in it better and stronger.

4

FOLKS WHO ARE GETTING IT RIGHT

This is the chapter I've been looking forward to writing the most, because I think it will be hopeful, encouraging, and instructive.

When I counsel interns about their education and moving toward a career in line with their passions and talents, I always give them this simple advice: Find the person or people who are successfully doing what you want to do, learn about their work, study it, and then call them up, tell them about your appreciation for their work and talk to them about where you are and learn how they got to where they are. As your relationship develops, see if you can develop a from-time-to-time mentoring relationship with them. They would be honored to be asked, and—unless it's someone like Bono or the president—it's very likely they would be most happy to make room for such a relationship.

So, one of the best educational experiences in life comes from carefully observing and learning from people who are successfully doing what you're interested in doing. And that is true for our topic. Whether you know a gay relative, coworker, or neighbor, you can learn much on how to develop good relationships by talking to others who have developed relationships with their LGBT neighbor. We are going to meet some of these people in this chapter. They are great, interesting, and creative folks and their stories run from the wonderfully everyday to the absolutely heroic.

Andrew and Christopher

Let me start with Andrew. We worked together for many years, were good friends, and I liked him primarily for his very dry but side-splitting sense of humor. He decided to take a midlife career shift and joined the pastoral staff of a good-sized church back home in Virginia. About the same time, he had the opportunity to reconnect with an old friend from their seminary days through Facebook. They were very close in school but had just lost touch. Like many such decades-gapped reunions, they enjoyed catching up with one another and learning what paths their lives had taken.

Andrew's friend Christopher had gone straight into successful pastoral ministry, but as usual, there were struggles. One of the biggest was with a dark secret deep in his heart. He had privately struggled with same-sex attraction from his early twenties, but believed going to seminary and throwing himself into the Lord's work would "snap him out of it." He found that plan a simplistic and illusory answer to a complex problem.

After many years of struggling with this and trying to be sincere in his ministry to his evangelical congregation, Christopher finally decided in his own mind to be honest, make the jump, accept his sexual reality, and live as a gay man. Still believing in his faith, he left his church and joined the ministry of a gay-affirming church. He said his life now seemed to make sense.

Andrew's response to his friend's life course was a friendly "WOW!" Christopher, in telling Andrew his story, concluded that that would be the last of their reconnecting, given Andrew's own life course. My friend asked Christopher, "Why would you think that?" to which Christopher replied, "Why would I *not* think that, given where you spent so many years working and where you work now? Don't forget, we went to seminary together. I know what you believe because I used to believe it too." Andrew asked to be given the benefit of any doubt.

Discovering that they coincidentally lived in neighboring towns, Andrew said he would very much like to get together and reconnect in a real way—not because he felt he had to prove Christopher wrong but because he was eager to see his old friend. So they met, and after some expected awkwardness, they fell back into how things were in their seminary days, discovering that despite taking different paths in life, they were still more alike than different. It was as if the passage of decades was merely months, picking right back up where they left off.

After a few more such get-togethers over lunches and dinners, each taking turns doing the traveling to each other's town, it was obvious to Christopher that Andrew was as theologically and socially conservative as he had ever been. But his beliefs and convictions about homosexuality had not come up, to Christopher's surprise. A big step for Christopher was when Andrew asked if he could take him by his church one day after lunch to introduce him to his staff and show him around their facility. Christopher later did the same with Andrew. Their relationship started to take a more committed turn when Christopher asked if they might do Bible study together as they had done in school. Andrew was both surprised and delighted, both for the trust and for the opportunity to take their relationship to a more substantive level.

So they meet together a few times a month, doing what Andrew described as "*real* Bible study," digging deep and unapologetically into the text, even those passages that might cause their relationship some trouble. As they both learned that either side of the relationship was not just for show or politeness, they felt comfortable enough to start talking

> After many years of trying to minister to his evangelical congregation, he finally decided to accept his reality and live as a gay man.

about their own convictions on the authority of Scripture, hermeneutics, what Christ demands of us in genuine discipleship, and the place sexuality plays in our lives and struggles.

Andrew tells me it is not always easy, that they do step on each other's toes here and there, but if it happens, they try to keep it to seriously held convictions rather than just thoughtlessness or lack of consideration. They have been meeting together for over a year now and count each other as valuable friends. They know there will always be this significant divide between them, but they are both committed to growing their relationship because of the regard they have for one another as well as what they are both learning about a world that's very different from their own, Andrew more so than Christopher. Andrew says this relationship has been a positive curiosity and discussion point with his peers at work, who watch the relationship develop with curiosity and have gained a new appreciation for seeking out similar out-of-the-box relationships themselves with, as Andrew jokingly explains, "bikers, atheists, and one went so far as to befriend a Democrat."

Walter, Kate, and Their Daughter, Julia

The Pinkstons live in a midsize Arkansas town where Walter has pastored the same Assemblies of God church for twenty-six years. Their three children grew up in this church, beloved by the congregation of just over 150 families, and "adopted" by a few of them as members of their own families. The two boys are in their late twenties and have both moved to nearby states for their work. Julia, in her early twenties, lives about twenty minutes from her parents. They have always been close, and Julia made it a point to establish her adult life so she could continue to live close to her parents. In her college years, Julia told her parents she had something difficult to talk to them about and could they make time in the next few days for them to discuss it. Concerned, her parents asked if she could come that night and they could all sit down together. She did.

Julia explained she had some news that would certainly surprise them and perhaps shock and disappoint them. She started by telling her parents how she had never really been comfortable around boys. Her parents said that, of course, they knew that. They assumed it was because Julia was more shy and bookish than most other girls, just more serious about life and focused on other things. Julia agreed that that was very much the case, but there was more to the story. She either didn't want to admit it or was unsure what her feelings really meant, but she recently had been forced to face the truth: she had romantic feelings for and sexual attractions to women. Obviously her parents were shocked by this news, but they comforted themselves by both thinking—independent from each other—that Julia was just confused as a young woman. They had not raised her to be that way, they told themselves. Her mom asked her how she could really be sure, and Julia kind of laughed nervously and answered, "Uh, I know what I feel, Mom. I'm pretty sure!"

The conversation was jarring for the Pinkstons, but they sought hope in the idea that regardless of what Julia said, this was probably a young-adulthood phase of searching and understanding. She would snap out of it after a while, they wanted to believe.

But Julia never did snap out of it. Curiously, the Pinkstons weren't angry, ashamed, or particularly happy for her. They just seemed to be indifferent, if not in denial about it. Kate wondered what the congregation would think if this news got out. Walter was not as concerned, because Julia was his daughter and he would always protect and stand by her side. Nothing could change that. They had seen another family demand their son leave their home when he admitted his same-sex desires to them. At the time, Walter and Kate believed that such a harsh response was wrong; and as shocked and even embarrassed as they were, they wanted Julia to know that this did not change one bit the bottomless love and appreciation they held for her.

One of Julia's brothers was not surprised by the news at all. He had sensed this was true of her since she was in her later teens and had come to terms with it on his own.

Her other brother reacted with harshness. The news itself was not a surprise to him, but he wondered why she needed to, as he put it, "make such a big deal about it!" He said he didn't feel the need to announce his sexual interests to the world and didn't know why she needed to. Kate told him it wasn't that simple and he should examine his attitude. But he continued to make his feelings known on the matter.

After some months, when Walter and Kate realized this was not likely to be a "phase," Walter decided he needed to share this family news with three of his trusted friends in the church, men whose leadership and judgment he relied on. To his surprise, two of the men were not shocked at all. In fact, Walt's news confirmed what they had suspected. They had seen Julia grow up, and she was considered a part of both families. The other friend wanted to know what it could have been in the way Walt and Kate raised Julia that could have led to this. To be honest, Walt said that he and Kate had thought about that a great deal and were not sure what that might be. Brad, one of the other two friends, told Walt not to play that game, that it probably wasn't anything he and Kate did or did not do. Brad assured Walt that all their children were really remarkable people. This made Walt feel good, but didn't erase those doubts.

As they worked through their own family feelings over the months, Walt and Kate asked Julia what she wanted to do regarding this news and their congregation. They believed, correctly, that that process was totally up to her. How did she want this news to be known, if at all? Julia told them that she didn't want it announced like it was some big thing, but neither did she want it hushed up. She told them she thought that the best thing was for them to talk about it with others as it naturally came up, just as if, she told them with a laugh, "I was becoming an amateur ornithologist." No reason to hide it or make a big deal about it.

And so the word slowly spread, and the three of them were actually surprised to see the reaction of the congregation and various individuals. For the most part, no one treated Julia any differently than they had, making Julia wonder who actually knew and who didn't. Many took their cues from Kate and Walter.

> "God has told me clearly that I deal with the same issue you do, perhaps even more so."

But what about the theology of their church, which their family had believed fully? None of them had any doubts or questions about what Scripture said about sexuality. Walt and Kate wondered how Julia would navigate this and how they would as well. No one brought it up until Julia expressed her desire to stay a part of "my congregation," as she put it, and wondered what effect that might have on the church and what her parents thought about that. Her father told her that he saw no reason why her same-sex attraction should exclude her from their congregation. But she knew that her father taught that the Scriptures said homosexuality was not God's design for His people, and how could they reconcile her staying in the church and their denomination's understanding of Scripture? Her wishes for remaining a part of her church conflicted with her sexual desires. She knew that.

One day as Walter and Julie were talking about this, Walter grabbed both of her hands in his, looked her in the eyes, and said, "Listen, Julia, I have been thinking and praying about this a great deal. It is not an easy one. But God has told me clearly that I deal with the same issue you do, probably even more so." A palpably confused look came across Julia's face. But Walter knew exactly what God meant, even if Julia didn't. Her father said, clasping her hands tighter with warmth and assurance:

"I cannot ignore or change what God says about His gift of sex. We have taught all you kids that as well as our congregation. But we all have sexual feelings that are contrary to God's good will for us. You are old enough to know this, that while I have always been faithful to your mother, I have struggled with physical desires for other women. Many men do. But it is a nearly daily battle for me to keep my mind clean in that regard and the fidelity of my heart to your mother and you kids intact. It is something I need to be honest about and constantly take to God. As well, we have plenty of single people in our church of all ages who are not able to realize their deepest sexual longings because God has not seen fit to bring them a spouse."

He continued, "We all have to bring these powerful desires obediently in line with God's will. It is not easy, but every Christian, including Jesus Himself, has had to deal with powerful temptations. Julia, am I a hypocrite because I have sexual temptations? Are the singles in our church wrong because they have sexual desires and attractions that they are not permitted to act upon? Should they be banned from the church? No, not as long as they seek to honor God's Word and His desire for us to live in obedience to Him. As long as you seek to live in that way, you are right in line, no worse, no better, than any other person in the body of Christ."

Even though Julia knows this is very difficult and even at times unfair, she knows it is not her dad's opinion, but the teachings of the faith she grew up in and that she loves. And she can either stay with it or leave it. But she knows it is not her place to change it. She is still unsure where she might land on the issue—choosing her church or another path.

Walter and Kate are thankful for Julia and are aware that not all stories turn out so harmoniously for parents and their children with same-sex attraction. And while this is not their motivator, they know it is no small thing how their congregation sees them as they stumble through this journey.

Sam and Nicole

Samantha is a twentysomething sales rep for a small company in Seattle that manufactures and sells medical devices to physician's offices.

She teaches a weekly Bible study for tween girls at the small Baptist church where she grew up. The congregation is very traditional, and so is Sam. On her sales team at work is Nicole, a very smart and professional woman about two years Sam's senior. They are both among the leaders of the "under-thirty" sales staff in terms of numbers and new client development, making them both a bit competitive with each other, but they try not to let that get in the way of their friendship. While similar in terms of professional reputation, they are as different as a duck and donkey in other ways. Sam was homeschooled her whole life while Nicole was "unschooled"—both innovative ways of gaining an education. As well, Sam is the "good Christian girl," while Nicole is an edgy and culturally sophisticated lesbian. Both, as they joke, help boost the company's diversity rating. Sam says that being in Seattle, she's the company's more prized diversity trophy while Nicole might as well be a "Walmart-shopping, football-watching, NASCAR-cheering white male."

Finding each other a curious oddity—country mouse and city mouse—they are both mature enough to be interested in and able to develop a meaningful friendship, one that some of their peers find intriguing and others peculiar. Nicole explains that her interest in Sam's friendship was rooted in professional respect but also the desire to get to know someone who was homeschooled, sexually conservative, and believed the Bible so seriously. "She might as well be Amish. I've heard of such people, but thought they all lived in Mississippi."

Sam's interest in Nicole came from the dissonance she experienced between what she assumed about lesbians and who Nicole actually is. Sam says, "She is so 'out, loud and proud' at work, but she's not obnoxious about it. I assumed that was required of all activists."

Nicole and Sam's relationship centers around three things primarily: work, their stark differences, and running. They run together nearly every day, either at lunch when not out on sales calls or before work at Robinswood Park. They have done three marathons together and countless shorter races. They are just as competitive here as they are at work. One is a vegan and the other eats no red meat, but does consume fish and some chicken. Surprisingly, Sam is the herbivore and Nicole is, as Sam ribs her, "the heartless flesh eater."

Their friendship is also a curiosity to their families who are both as far apart from each other as the polar ice caps. But they have come to see that their daughters value and have grown through their relationship, and that makes them happy.

Shane and Dan

Dan Cathy was thrown headfirst into the deep end of the culture war on the homosexuality debate. He's the president and CEO of one of the most successful and faithfully frequented fast-food chains in the United States, Chick-fil-A. In twin interviews on a radio show and then an online Christian news site a few years ago, Cathy explained the company's well-known corporate values: "We are very much supportive of the family—the biblical definition of the family unit," and that we invite God's judgment as a nation when we say we have a better understanding of what marriage is than He does.

Not a radical or controversial statement to most people, but it set the match to a national firestorm, gaining his company the dubious accusation of being bigoted and hateful. Major newspapers, television networks, and media commentators fanned the flames as the interview with Cathy started to spread with what to them were self-evident accusations about gay people. Mayors of a few northern cities declared Chick-fil-A *persona non grata*, ceremoniously unwelcome in their cities. Student groups worked to get the company's food service kicked off the campus's student centers. It is surprising to many that Cathy did not say anything—either good or bad—about homosexuality in his comments, only that his company supported the "biblical definition of the family unit." That was deemed hate speech by much of the cultural elite.

I've had the opportunity of meeting Dan Cathy and his brother

Don (who goes by "Bubba") a few times, and they are both notably humble, mild-spoken, and kind. You would never pick them out of a crowd as the billionaires and corporate mavens they are. There is not an ounce of pretense or pride in them. Nearly everyone who meets Dan has the same impression, even Shane Windmeyer.

Shane is one of the founders and current executive director of Campus Pride, a national organization dedicated to encouraging and creating "safer, more inclusive LGBT-friendly colleges and universities," as their mission statement explains. His organization had been a key player in protesting and working to remove Chick-fil-A as a vendor on many college campuses.

> "Dan Cathy expressed genuine sadness when he heard of people being treated unkindly in the name of Chick-fil-A, but he offered no apologies for his beliefs about marriage."

In 2012, Shane got a call on his cellphone from a very unlikely source: Dan Cathy. Wondering if he was going to be informed that the Chick-fil-A lawyers were coming after him, he anxiously took the call. It was the exact opposite of what he expected. Shane explained that the first call "lasted over an hour and the private conversation led to more calls the next week and the week after." They began texting as well. Cathy was interested in learning what he could about Shane as a person —who he was, why he did the work he did, and what his strongest-held convictions were about.

These early connections soon led to in-person meetings where Shane was able to meet other representatives of Dan's company. Shane relates that Dan "had never before had such dialogue with any member of the LGBT community," and "it was awkward at times, but always genuine and kind." He was surprised and impressed that Dan "expressed a sincere interest in my life, wanting to get to know me on a personal level. He wanted to know about where I grew up, my faith, my family, even my husband, Tommy. In return, I learned about his wife and kids and gained an appreciation for his devout faith and his commitment to being a 'follower of Christ' more than a 'Christian.' "

Shane also reported that "Dan expressed regret and genuine sadness when he heard of people being treated unkindly in the name of Chick-fil-A, but he offered no apologies for his genuine beliefs about marriage."

On this last point, Shane explains with clarity, respect, and honesty:

> Dan, in his heart, is driven by his desire to minister to others and had to choose to continue our relationship throughout this controversy. He had to both hold to his beliefs and welcome me into them. He had to face the issue of respecting my viewpoints and life even while not being able to reconcile them with his belief system. He defined this to me as "the blessing of growth." He expanded his world without abandoning it. I did, as well.[1]

The biggest shocker came later. Shane was invited to attend Chick-fil-A's largest event of the year as Dan and his family's personal guest: the annual New Year's Eve Chick-fil-A Bowl in Atlanta. A little concerned that he might be being played by such a significant invitation, Shane went with some hesitation, but realized Dan was putting something on the line as well in his own community by extending the invitation. On the night of the football game, Dan and his family stood on the sidelines with Shane the whole night, happy and proud to have one of their new friends enjoy the evening with them.

Shane and Dan's relationship is as good as any I could have imagined to bring to life the message and intention of this book. But while

---

1. Shane Windmeyer, "Dan and Me: My Coming Out as a Friend of Dan Cathy and Chick-fil-a," *Huffington Post Gay Voices*, January 28, 2013.

Dan did not face any notable blowback from the Christian community, and thankfully mostly encouragement and appreciation, Shane was not so fortunate. He's taking heat from a few of his own for entering into a friendship with the likes of Dan, standing "up for them and defending their hatred" because it's Dan who "should be the one putting out statements in support of LGBTQ youth, not the other way around" as one of Shane's critics asserted in the Huffington Post's *Gay Voices* blog. This criticism of Shane is unfortunate and undeserved because principled civility is a noble thing. And kudos to him for being in and valuing this friendship in the face of challenges from his peers. That's both mature and a sign of character.

Htoo and His Employees

Htoo (Hit-to) lives in Santa Monica, California, and owns a mid-level film production company that produces documentaries for international clients. Htoo is profoundly creative, smart, and conservatively Catholic. With a staff his size in the trade he's in, he has a number of gay and lesbian employees, which, as he does all his employees, he loves and deeply appreciates. He is very close to two in particular by nature of their personal interests and personalities. Bethany is a very serious surfer, as is Htoo, and they both enjoy sneaking out of the office when the waves are up and catch some time together in the break. Having an office right on the Pacific Coast Highway means they can go from their desks to paddling out in about five minutes.

The second, Derek, shares a passion with Htoo for US Civil War history. Yes! Not to the extreme of being Civil War reenactors, as there are not that many opportunities for such activity in the Los Angeles area. But they are quite serious in studying up and seeking to outdo each other in rare books collected and new facts to share on the subject. They've even visited a number of famous sites together; last year being Vicksburg, Mississippi.

While Bethany, Derek, and the other gay and lesbian employees would not call Htoo's production company a "gay-friendly workplace" in the political sense, it is certainly a friendly atmosphere for them. And in the world of documentary filmmaking, being employed there is no small thing to have on one's resume.

A few years ago, Htoo and a number of his employees—gay and straight—came to a difficult spot in their relationship. Quite rough. During the very contentious and polarizing Proposition 8 effort in California—a citizen proposition on how legal marriage would be defined in the Golden State—the employees wondered whether their company would get involved in the effort financially. And if so, the big question would be, in which way?

Many of the employees knew Htoo's faith convictions as a Catholic, but were sure he would never support, financially or otherwise, an effort they saw as draconian and prejudicially motivated against the gay community. They imagined, given their understanding of the measure, that he might even be willing to donate financially to their side of the issue, given his regard for them. "How could someone as progressive and considerate as Htoo not oppose such a discriminatory effort?" they wondered.

So they approached him about where their company would stand on the issue. Htoo imagined such a conversation would be coming and he'd been praying about how to handle it. When the request was made from his employees, Htoo carefully listened to each person and tried his best to understand and put himself in their place, seeing the issue from their perspective. As a few made their case, Htoo took a long pause and said he would be forthright with them.

He defined his perspective on the issue and why he thought it was important that marriage remain what it has been in all cultures in all places at all time, a union that joined the two parts of humanity together. He did so from both a faith and social perspective. His general convictions on this were not news to anyone on his team, given his faith and view of the world. But it did cause them concern in where he might be going with this.

Htoo then explained at the meeting that he had been giving this issue much thought because of its importance to the future of the family. He told all that he hoped that it was clear he deeply valued and loved each member of his team, regardless of what their story was, affirming them as people and counting them among his closest friends. And he trusted he could count on the same kind of regard from them, given who he was.

He gave them his decision. The company would not be involved in the issue, sitting out taking one side or the other, explaining that as the owner of this company, he believed God had entrusted it to him and he had the responsibility of honoring Him with it. Therefore, he had to take a contrary position. But he also knew what this issue meant to many of his employees, and recognized it would be difficult for them knowing that their workplace supported something they saw as harmful to them and their friends. It allowed Htoo not to violate his conscience, but also not hurt his employees.

He explained that even though he had dear friends in this company and throughout their professional community who took a different view, he obviously had his own strongly held convictions. And therefore, he was going to support the Prop 8 effort as a citizen with his own money and he assumed that they would oppose the effort as citizens with their own money.

The room had become noticeably uncomfortable. A few spoke up angrily, asking if Htoo understood what message this was sending to each gay and lesbian employee of the company, as well as the LGBT-friendly straights.

He assured them he understood both the larger and personal politics of the issue and he regretted it had become such a divisive issue. He then asked if they could understand how someone might hold

> He expressed his deep desire that they could all coexist as friends and colleagues in spite of their differing views.

a differing position based on one's conviction on what marriage is and should remain rather than any ill will against gay and lesbian people. He then added, "I hope my long friendship with and unconditional esteem for everyone on our team is evidence enough that I am not motivated by any antigay sentiments in this, just like I don't see your disagreement with my faith and personal convictions an indication that you are prejudiced or unwilling to accept me or people of faith."

He ended by expressing his deep desire that they could all continue to coexist as friends and colleagues in spite of their differing views on this significant issue. The emotional and relational dust in the office did not settle for some time, but Htoo was committed to doing what he could do at backing up his care for and appreciation of his friends and employees with real kindness and genuine friendship. He says things have gotten better with the team, and he is glad for that.

Esperanza and Her Son's Partner

Esperanza is a regular, everyday person but also a living, breathing incarnation of Christ in her small part of the world. Decades ago, her son came out to the whole family, announcing that he was a homosexual. As a Christian mother, she was devastated, ashamed, and totally unsure of what to do. Her countless efforts to "talk her son straight" had no effect. She could not accept her son's understanding of himself, not with her mind nor her heart.

Years later, she got an evening job waiting tables at a restaurant. Her boss asked her if she realized the diner was a "gay hangout" at night. It looked like a regular short-order establishment to her, but feeling that

God had led her to the job, she stuck it out. She applied herself to her work and came to love the men who came in every night.

Years later her son, Tony, now a young adult, moved in with his partner, an older man whom his friends called "Sage." Given her many years at the diner, she came to be able to connect with people she never thought she could, even as she remained the Christian she always had been. She tried to befriend Sage but he was not kind to Esperanza, saying disturbing things about sex and God to shock and embarrass her polite Christian sensibilities. Esperanza also learned that Sage had infected her only son with HIV and that they both had contracted full-blown AIDS.

> "Sage was not the enemy. He was another lost soul created in the image of God, just like my son."

She wrestled with the hatred and anger she felt toward Sage for the death sentence he had given her boy, but then she remembered what she had learned years earlier by working with the young gay men at the diner. Esperanza came to understand, "Sage was not the enemy. He was another lost soul created in the image of God, just like my son."

This changed her whole perspective toward both her son and his partner in a supernatural way. She committed herself to loving and caring for the man who infected her son. In time, Sage's health started to decline dramatically. Bedridden, he had no one to care for him, not his family who rejected him or his friends. Esperanza stepped up, realizing that this is what Jesus would have her do. She fed and cleaned him, tracked his medications, and changed his diapers. In the midst of all this, he still taunted her, but by now this only increased her compassion for him. "He must be so unhappy inside to be so mean on the outside," she told herself.

She continued to do these difficult daily tasks of care for Sage as a sign of love toward him and her son. She also spent time just talking and being with him, learning about his family and his childhood. In time, Sage came to love Esperanza, and they shared many sweet moments together as he slid into his sad, slow, and agonizing death. Sage is gone and Tony is living with AIDS, but he knows in a very powerful way that even though his mother holds to her Christian convictions, there is no doubt she now has a great love in her heart for people like him. She demonstrated it with Sage and continues to with his other friends in ways he cannot really understand.

Conclusion

These stories are only the tip of the iceberg of such encouraging relationships. They are all around you. Look for them, learn from them.

5

NAVIGATING THE DILEMMAS WE FACE IN OUR FRIENDSHIPS

Imagine you're driving around a massively large city you've never been to before: Shanghai, China. It's like nothing you've ever seen and therefore quite intimidating and overwhelming for the uninitiated. You're assigned a mission to find a number of locations throughout the city, but you have no map and no one to guide you. Obviously, you're in a bit of a pickle. You're not sure how to find what you're looking for and you don't know the local customs and rules, so you don't want to unwittingly offend the locals as you go about your mad search, thus needlessly complicating the already impossible task.

Anyone navigating unfamiliar territory needs a guide, some basic knowledge of and wisdom about the local geographical layout, the community customs, and the language. And so we need to learn to navigate the highways and byways of making and maintaining friendships with those who hold very different beliefs from our own, be they people with differing sexual mores, beliefs about God, taste in music, or political leanings.

In the next three chapters, we will explore a host of relational situations that many of us face currently or will soon as we build and maintain meaningful and healthy relationships with our LGBT friends, neighbors, family members, and those who come to our churches. These are unfamiliar territories for those of us on both sides of the issue, requiring some guidance and orientation. So let's get a map and try to make sense of where we want to go.

Should I Respond to and Treat All Gay and Lesbian People the Same?

The answer to the above question is other than what you might think: *Not necessarily.* This seems like a strange and even unjust answer, as all people, even our LGBT neighbors, are created in and bear the very image of God in who and what they are. Why shouldn't we respond to and treat each of them equally? Well, in one sense we certainly should, given this fundamental truth of their divine image-bearing nature.

Yet there is another level to this answer that matters if we are to understand this issue with the complexity it involves. This other level is most certainly true for *all* people and not just our gay and lesbian neighbors and friends. We do not and should not respond to and treat all people the same—save for basic respectfulness, kindness, and helpfulness—for there are very important differences among us all that have nothing to do with our individual value and worth. To treat everyone the same is to fail to recognize their uniqueness, personality, natures, and the nature of their relationship with us. Here's one for instance:

All people have different temperaments, spirits, and personalities. It's what makes life with others more interesting. Some we can be very frank with; others need more tender treatment. Some have a great sense of humor. Others, not so much. Some are by nature combative; others tend to be agreeable. Some have sensitive spirits; others are rock-hard, even seemingly unfeeling. I have a dear friend who has the unique gift of making you feel good and at ease by being hard with you. Her husband says he knows when she doesn't care for someone—because she's so nice to them.

So it is with gay and lesbian people. Each is to be seen as the person they are, in their complexity, difference, and wonder, rather than "Frank, the gay guy" or "Beverly, the lesbian." The starting place is, "Frank is Frank" and "Beverly is Beverly." You wouldn't want to be known as "Jimmy, the Tongues-Talking Pentecostal" or "Sandra, the Five-Point Calvinist," would you?

But there's another angle that is specific to interacting with different gay and lesbian individuals either as friends or random folks out in the culture. One particular set of guides has been provided by Kevin DeYoung, a wise and biblically faithful pastor of a campus church at the University of Michigan in Lansing. He asks the question, "So when speaking to homosexuals, should we be defiant and defensive or gentle and entreating?" His answer? *Yes and yes*, explaining it depends on who's listening.

This might seem contradictory, but it speaks to the balance of grace and truth and recognizing and honoring the individual or group we are speaking to and taking them seriously for who they are and what they are about.

DeYoung explains:

- If we are speaking to cultural elites who are antagonistic toward Christians and our beliefs, we want to be gracious and patient but also bold and courageous.
- If we are speaking to those struggling in resisting their same-sex attraction, we want to be patient and sympathetic.
- If we are speaking to sufferers who have been mistreated by the church, we want to be humbly apologetic and healing.
- If we are speaking to shaky Christians who seem ready to compromise the faith for society's approval, we want to be faithfully persuasive and persistent.

- If we are speaking to liberal Christians who have deviated from the truth once delivered for the saints, we want to be serious and hortatory.
- If we are speaking to gays and lesbians who live as the Scriptures would not have them live, we want to be winsome and straightforward.
- If we are speaking to belligerent Christians who hate or fear homosexuals, we want to be upset, disappointed, and corrective.[1]

I would add another important one:

- If we are speaking to homosexuals who are seeking to live obediently and faithfully to orthodox Christian discipleship and its sexual ethics, we must be encouraging and helpful.

Regarding these different ways of interacting with various folks, an approach I have taken in my work and relationships in general is to accept and treat everyone you meet as a potential new friend until they give you unavoidable reason to do otherwise. And we must be long-suffering before coming to that conclusion.

I will usually have people come up to me after a speaking event to challenge me on a part or the whole of what I have said. I welcome and honestly enjoy these exchanges. In these instances, I will introduce myself, ask their name, and shake their hand as a gesture of kindness and respect toward them. I have had people refuse to shake my hand. Such people should still be treated graciously, but they have clearly communicated how they want to be treated and engaged: from a distance. And

---

1. Kevin DeYoung, "The Church and Homosexuality: Ten Commitments," *The Gospel Coalition*, May 30, 2012, http://thegospelcoalition.org/blogs/kevindeyoung/ 2012/05/30/the-church-and-homosexuality-ten-commitments/.

that must be respected, regardless of how you feel about it. However, most times I have those who want to challenge and really press me hard, doing so with civility, respect, and often a "thank you for coming" and a gracious handshake. They have communicated as well how they want to interact, and I'm always thankful for it.

QUESTIONS AND ANSWERS
In Dealing with Our Friends

Friendships are unarguably one of the most important spices of life. But unfortunately, not enough hold to the idea that the more diverse the relationships, the more interesting. I get to travel a good bit internationally, and therefore have many friends from different parts of the world, but I wish I had more in my daily, local life. I wish I had more friends who work in the arts, are leather clad bikers or skaters, bibliophiles, atheists, gardeners, existentialists, nutritionists, magicians, street performers. All kinds of interesting people. But it is good for us to break out of our homogenous communities and be challenged and educated. So let's address some questions relative to our topic.

1. *Can we become friends? Should we?*

Yes and yes. And to quote Forrest Gump: *That's all I got to say about that.*

2. *Should we become friends to share the gospel?*

Just as direct: No!

Should we share the gospel? Of course, just as we should with all. It is Christ's command to us.

But we don't develop friendships with people for that reason alone, or even primarily. In fact, to do so is not a friendship; it's a project, and no one wants to be someone's project. And we won't typically be effective in sharing Christ's redeeming love with anyone if that is our only interest in them. There are so many stories of people turning their lives over to Jesus, not because they were logically convinced of the truth of Christianity or because a certain presentation was so compelling, but because the telling of the gospel was first established upon and backed up by an undeniable caring and self-giving friendship.

We cannot fully see someone as a divine and God-loved image-bearer if we see them only as a sales prospect for evangelism efforts. That objectifies them, and who likes that? Put yourself in their place, which is always a good quality of any friendship. Would you like to be befriended solely for the purposes of accepting another's beliefs? Besides, people have a pretty good sense of whether they are really being befriended or set up for a sales pitch, whether it be a multilevel marketing opportunity or a conversion to your faith.

Be friends first. Then as the relationship develops and matures, naturally talk about why your faith matters to you and be open to understanding why their beliefs are important to them. This is what friends do: they want to know what makes the other tick, what's important to them and why. And in good friendships, that happens naturally.

3. *What should they expect of me?*

This is a very important question and the best answers, as most will be, are not specific to developing friendships with our LGBT neighbors. And that is the first truth we must know. This relationship is like any other relationship you would pursue with anyone else. And it might go somewhere, and it might not, like any initiation toward a friendship. That's how relationships work.

Healthy and growing relationships are generally centered on common interests and a genuine interest and appreciation for the person you are befriending. This is a non-negosh. Other expectations your friends will have are:

- that you care for them, with no strings attached. Friends for friendship's sake.
- that you be yourself, as much as is proper for the age and development of your relationship.
- that you be willing to put yourself out a bit in terms of your comfort zone, willing to enter their world in reasonable and acceptable ways.
- that you will be there for them as much as you possibly can, appropriate to the nature of your relationship. (Clinginess is never good.)
- that you be patient with them regarding the newness, uncertainty, and disagreement inherent in such relationships, which there are in *any* relationship.
- that you let them be themselves.
- that your differences are not what define the relationship.
- that you let them have their own convictions as everyone has a right to believe "wrong" things. You do and your friends do. But this does not mean that you can't or shouldn't talk about them from time to time and challenge one another. This is what good, honest, and trusting friends do as well.
- that you rejoice with them, as much as possible, over their joys and mourn with them over their losses.
- that you will be truthful with them, at appropriate times and in appropriate ways.

4. What should you expect of them?

All of the same things; however, you should be more patient and forgiving if and when your friend is not able to or doesn't always relate accordingly. Relationships are a two-way street, and a good friend always tries to forgive and not demand too much. But a good friend and a healthy person doesn't let themselves be abused or run over. That goes both ways.

5. When do I tell them they're wrong?

Of course, if this is an objective, you aren't interested in friendship. You are interested in delivering a sermon. *When do you want them to tell you* you're *wrong?*

But that doesn't mean the subject will not or should never come up. Think of it just as you would in any other relationship, between a vegetarian and a carnivore, a libertarian and a socialist, an Alabama fan and an Auburn fan. No friendship can or should lead with its differences, but neither do they ignore them.

First, it is unlikely you need to state the obvious. You know what their story is and they know what yours is. I've never told any of my LGBT friends that I think homosexuality is wrong. Never had to. They are a perceptive bunch, picking up on such vibes given my writings, my work, and my approach to my faith. I know where they're coming from also.

But the topic will and should come up as the relationship matures. It will arise naturally, and while it shouldn't be pressed in an unnatural way, it shouldn't be ignored or avoided. Good friends deal with differences honestly, kindly, and hopefully in a spirited way, for it's really only in friendship where this can truly happen. This is because we are more secure with each other, we know the weaknesses in each other's positions, and the relationship can withstand that heat. This is the nature of friendships. It's why Thanksgiving dinners with the family can be so spirited. We are too tied together to bail on one another, even if that's exactly what we feel like doing. And actually, that's a great friendship, isn't it?

But both have to be mindful of the maturity and strength of the relationship and act accordingly.

6. Do I need to meet and spend time with their friends?

Hanging with each other's friends can be a very fun and exciting part of any friendship; you get to enter into and explore new worlds as they actually are. As with most friendships, you should be open and willing to get to know your friend's friends. And, as with any other relationship, you don't have to like them. They might not be your kind of people.

I have a very dear friend who actually likes Weird Al Yankovic. No, not just tolerates him—likes him. He listens to Weird Al by his own choosing. And yes, he's a grown man with otherwise good taste. And our relationship can and does withstand this one lapse. But if he introduced me to his other Weird Al friends, I would feel no compulsion or desire to like them, much less be friends with them. And as close as we are, I wouldn't feel bad about telling him, "Leon, your friends are weirdos!" We don't have to like everyone, even if they are our friends' friends. And they don't have to like ours. But most of the time, we like to meet our friends' friends and often make cherished new friendships through these introductions.

You should be willing to meet some of their good friends and help them feel comfortable in meeting yours. Of course, you want to make sure you are introducing them to the right friends of yours, those they would actually enjoy meeting. You would hope they'd do the same for you.

It has been important for me to meet my gay and lesbian friends' partners, as these are important people in their lives. And like any other such relationship, it's normal for us to evaluate that partner in relation to our friend. It is natural—and not judgmental—to say to ourselves "Wow, she seems very nice" or "Sheez, what are they thinking? He must have money." My buddy John's partner is Mark. He is a lawyer who worked for many years in the auto industry. I was really surprised that when I met Mark, I liked him a lot. Later I told John that I actually liked Mark better than I liked him. Of course, he took it as a deep compliment, as any of us would. And as with anyone else we encounter, it is normal to evaluate them based on the kind of person they are.

I have really wanted some of my gay and lesbian friends to meet some of my Christian friends and have been able to arrange such introductions because I want them to meet Christians who beautifully

> "Can I give you a hug?" she said to me. "I've never hugged someone from the religious right!"

defy the stereotypes. John and I worked it out for him to come and visit me in my city and come to work and meet my colleagues. The day before he was to come, my father passed away and I had to rush home to Pensacola. John wondered what he should do, and I told him he should still come, that he would be in very good hands with my friends. I so hated that I missed his visit, but he enjoyed his time and was cared for and hosted very well by my friends. I was very happy for that. Things like this are good for my gay and lesbian friends, just as it has been good for me to meet their friends. It busts the stereotypes that I have. However, sometimes both introductions reinforce them. That is how people are.

I remember one particularly pleasant meal I had with a friend's colleagues from his campus LGBT group at a large university in North Carolina. They were a fun bunch. One of the folks at the table was transgendered, in the midst of his transition to presenting as a female. She was a bit awkward in herself, learning how to manage her lipstick, jewelry, and other such female accessories. However, she didn't let that bother her.[2] She was very kind and gregarious. We enjoyed talking, and she was very forward in asking me about where I worked with very precise questions. She apologized for her interrogation, but I told her I didn't mind at all. In fact, I appreciated her honest interest. When our collective time was over, we stood, said our goodbyes, and she asked me, "Can

---

2. Another issue that one must consider in relationships with transgendered people is what pronouns to use. Some people insist on using pronouns that correspond to a transgendered person's natural gender, refusing to recognize the feelings and changes that led to their present state. Of course, there is a valid reason for this, recognizing and respecting God's design of that person. I have decided for myself to use pronouns in line with how these people understand themselves to be, surely not due to any compromise on the matter, but simply out of consideration for the person and the facilitation of smoother interaction with them.

I give you a hug goodbye? I've never hugged someone from the religious right!" We all laughed and I told her of course, and that it would be the first for me as I'd never hugged a woman who used to be a man.

I took her comment as an indication of our sense of comfort and familiarity with each other. She did the same thing with mine. Such would not typically be appropriate with folks who had met just before lunch, but in this case it worked.

7. What if I offend them?

Trust me, the question is not *if* but *when*.

It's inevitable. I had a joint speaking event with a friend at the university where he is a professor. As we were making plans about my coming, he kindly invited me to stay at his house with him and his partner. I was honored and accepted without hesitancy. As the day for my departure drew close, my wife asked me about the trip. I gave her the details: my flight, how long I'd be gone, and my housing invitation. She agreed it was important for our relationship to stay with them but asked what my bosses at work would think about that, given that it was a work trip. Good question. I said I was sure they'd be fine with it. She wisely said I should check to make sure, so I did.

What would *you* think is the right decision in such a situation? Suppose *you* work for a major Christian ministry and live a bit of a public life. You get such an invitation from a valued friend and you want to honor that kindness. Would you have accepted the invitation? What would the best response from your boss be? There is no clear answer at the back of this book. It's one of those gray areas where an objective right or wrong doesn't exist, only a judgment call.

Well, here's what happened in this case. I asked a few key leaders at the ministry before I asked my boss. I just wanted to get their advice and feel for the situation. Did they see it the way I did? Interestingly, some said, "What's the question? Of course you should!" while others I respected said, "I don't think it's wise from appearances. If it got out, some might exploit it and others might not understand."

But, of course, my boss was the one who counted, as I was under his authority. He was pretty straightforward: *no*. I respected him and honored his direction. I could see where he was coming from, but I was disappointed and not just because I had to call my friend and explain it to him. It wasn't going be an easy discussion, and I didn't want to offend him or hurt his feelings.

I explained my situation the best I could, saying I had to respectfully honor the authority I was under. He was very hurt and honest in telling me so. I know he was looking forward to showing me hospitality. I tried to explain to him—clumsily—that it wasn't about him and his partner, which he couldn't help but believe was exactly the problem.

I suggested we set aside time when I arrived to get a long lunch and talk it over. We did, over our favorite sushi, and I was very pleased that it did go very well. In thinking about it on my flight there, I realized a way to explain the truth, that it was not about his homosexuality per se, or them personally, even though he couldn't imagine how it could not be. I explained that whether he could believe it or not, it would be the same if he and his partner were a heterosexual cohabiting couple. The situation was contrary to the sexual ethic we hold and therefore was not wise for me to participate in, even though it was a gracious and innocent offer. That explanation helped a bit, but it was not pleasant for either of us. However, we worked through it with honesty and our best effort at understanding, and I was impressed and grateful for how he came to understand the position I was in, as well as my appreciation for him. It strengthened our relationship, but not without it "walking with a limp" for a while. Such things are bound to happen and it is a test of the relationship and each other's maturity.

In any relationship where there are significant differences in general perspectives, ideas, values, nationalities, or ethnicities, there is going to be some level of offense. It comes with the territory of entering unfamiliar worlds. And friendships learn how to deal with them.

Here's another story. A lesbian friend who works in the media in New York City asked me a year or two ago what I thought about the "pray-the-gay-away" approach to homosexuality. That is exactly what she said, and it offended me because it takes something very serious and complex and presents it in a cartoonish way. How did I react? I asked her to explain to me just what that meant. She looked at me curiously as if to say, "You know exactly what I mean." I purposely didn't take the cue. I wanted her to explain what she meant so that I could give her a good explanation of what I really thought concerning the topic of whether change and spiritual transformation are possible for those who desire it. I let her know I wasn't going to play that game and explained why such language was both offensive and uninformed.

Christians must appreciate that there are some small things that people (Christians and otherwise) can tend to say mindlessly but are hurtful to our LGBT friends. Some of them are:

- *"The gay lifestyle."* While even certain gay writers and leaders use this phrase, it can be offensive to some because it portrays their sexuality as a club they signed up for, a fad they are following, or a philosophy they adhere to. A lifestyle could be living at Venice Beach, loving to sail, being a bow hunter, or a Martha Stewart devotee. One's sexuality is typically deeper than that.
- *"Love the sinner, hate the sin."* The second part of this statement tends to cancel out the first. They don't typically see their sexual relationships as sin, so the first part is not good news. That would be like atheists saying to Christians, "Love the irrational, hate the irrationality." They mean well, and think they are actually being gracious, but it doesn't hit those they are talking to very well. On top of this, catchy phrases, as true as they might seem, are not typically helpful because they tend to trivialize what they try to explain. Don't use

them, regardless of who you are talking to.

- *"They choose to be that way..."* We addressed this in chapter 3, the false choice between "born that way" or "choose it." Like the "pray-the-gay-away" line, it is a horrible and false simplification of a complex issue. And such a statement goes into the ears of the same-sex-attracted person as "I have no idea about your story and don't really want to."

8. *What if they can't accept my faith?*

What if? What if you don't accept their view on sexuality? It's very likely you won't. And it's likely that they won't.

To base the future or nature of a friendship on such a thing is conditional and therefore not a relationship. It is like the earlier story of the anthropology grad student and her bisexual friend. There were unrealistic conditions put on that relationship, actually disqualifying it as a real friendship.

But here is what's reasonable. Any real friend should respect your adherence to and convictions about your faith. And you should do the same with them and their convictions. You could have a Buddhist friend. You don't have to agree with their faith. You might even think it is weird or incomprehensible. But this person is your friend, a friendship you have entered into willingly, in good faith, and it means something to you. You can disagree with their faith. You can debate with them about it and them with you. But a friend is respectful about what the other holds dear and how they voice their disagreements. Friends don't avoid differences, but they should disagree in caring ways.

6

NAVIGATING THE DILEMMAS WE FACE IN OUR HOMES AND CHURCHES

Typically our home and church are places of love, hope, and joy. Our family and church friends support and comfort us, and hopefully we give them comfort and support as well. In the midst of these places of refuge, it is quite possible family members and church guests will enter who have also entered the homosexual community. How do we respond to them?

Home is one of the toughest places to know how to engage a gay or lesbian family member in grace and truth because it's in our families where we tend to have the longest, closest, and most emotionally intense—for good or ill—relationships in our lives. Home is where we need acceptance the most. Home is where we have the highest expectations of others. Home is really where we are stuck with each other, and thankfully so. And many families deal with these issues of sexual difference in very intimate ways, with siblings, children, cousins, aunts, uncles, and even parents who announce their homosexuality or desire for a sex change later in life. It can be a bomb that's dropped in the middle of a family. That's why the "coming-out" process and experience is such a big and often terrifying thing to those who do it.

Major Questions Families Have

In this section, we will address some of the major questions that family members have about their gay loved ones.

1. *How should I love my gay child?*

For many years, Focus on the Family ran conferences around the nation every year, helping thousands of families learn how to deal with this issue in their homes in truthful and gracious ways. We would get the most heart-wrenching letters from attendees on how the conference had helped them in what seemed like, at that time, a hopeless situation. It was very humbling, and the people who actually did the hands-on work were tremendously gifted with deep hearts for those we were reaching. One comment we got back, from a mother whose son came out to their family in the last year, was a remarkably painful comment for the team, even though it was good news. She told a group of us after the conference, "Thank you for giving me permission to love my gay son!"

I felt a sharp emotional stab right through my gut. And I felt immediate compassion for her. Why that reaction? I thought, "Oh my goodness, where did you ever get the idea that you couldn't love your gay child? Who influenced you with such a horrible lie?"

But there are many instances of parent/child relationships that don't turn out like this one. I cannot imagine how any parent could respond this way, but many young adult children who have come out to their parents are told, "You are no longer our child and we hope you have a good life." Boom. Done. Out!

Too often Christian parents do this, but it is also frequently just run-of-the-mill parents who cannot accept, much less continue to love, such a child. That's your *child*!

To say it is shameful is an understatement. In fact, I am hard-pressed to find the appropriate words to denounce such a course of action by any family member.

So should you continue to love your gay child? For the Christian parent, there is only one answer. Did the waiting father Jesus told us about in His parable continue to love his wayward son? The whole point of Jesus' parable was that this father's love for his son was lavish, and could we say ridiculously so? His joy was in that his son returned and repented of his waywardness!

You might think this story has nothing to do with your situation because your son or daughter has not repented and doesn't seem anywhere close to doing so. Well, there's more to the story here. Read it in its fullness in Luke 15. On the return of the prodigal son to his father's house, we read: "And he arose and came to his father. But while he was still a long way off, his father saw him and felt compassion, and ran and embraced him and kissed him. And the son said to him, 'Father, I have sinned against heaven and before you. I am no longer worthy to be called your son'" (vv. 20–21).

Do you note something important here? It's in the order of events. It begins, "But while he was a long way off. . . ."

Two things here. First, his father spotted him at a distance. The father had most likely been looking constantly at the horizon, probably many times a day for the hope of his son's return. Second, the main action of the story happened while the son "was still a long way off." This marks something key about the story, but seldom appreciated. Jesus tells us plainly what that is: "But while he was still a long way off, his father saw him and felt compassion, and ran and embraced him and kissed him."

With the son so far off, the father couldn't know why the son was returning. Was he coming home with hat in hand, remorseful for his sins, to get more "stuff," or just to come back home because his fun ran out? Apparently the father didn't care, only that he *was* returning. And the sight of his son immediately filled his heart with compassion and joy regardless of why he was returning.

So this wealthy nobleman pulled up the front of his robe for speed and *ran* to his son. He didn't wait for the son to get to him. *He ran to him.* Men of such social stature did not run. They didn't exert any such energy. They had others do it for them. But the return of his son essentially caused him to lose all mindfulness of his social status and the expectations associated with it. He only cared about one thing: his son who was now back home.

But the son was repentant of his sins and said he was not even worthy to be his son any longer and asked if he could be taken back as a hired hand. And while repentance is essential for our Father's forgiveness and redemption, it is not a requirement for His deep love for us. That has always existed and always will, regardless of what we do. And we, as Christian parents, are to follow the same example the best we can in our limited ways.

> We are to love our gay children lavishly and unconditionally, because they are our children.

How should we love our gay children? Lavishly and unconditionally, because they are our children. To do so is not to compromise our Christian faith, by no means, but to fulfill it.

But as we will see, there is a difference between lovingly and passionately accepting our children and accepting or winking at their sin. We are not allowed to wink at anyone's sin, including our own or our loved ones'. Is this unfair or hard to do? Not really, for if we will take notice of it, we do this with people all the time, for no friends, family members, or loved ones agree on every all-important and consequential things or live sinless lives. We accept others as loved ones while also disagreeing with particular parts of their lives. Uncle Buck beds a number of women regularly. We don't like it. We don't think it's good or right. But he's still Uncle Buck. He's ours.

This is a part of all relationships and certainly not any kind of moral compromise. Uncle Buck knows how you feel about his sexual habits. You might talk to him about it from time to time, but there's no reason to make it a dividing line between you. And there is no reason to bring it up nearly every time you see him. People who do such things are what everyone would call a "pest." Isn't it true that we hope others will love us in spite of the things we do that they don't agree with? Otherwise we would only have friends and loved ones who agree perfectly with us on all-important issues. There are two words to describe people with such expectations: lonely and pharisaical.

2. *What about her/his partner?*

So we might think, "I will always love my son or daughter, but I don't have to love that person they are doing heaven knows what with!"

Should you love this person? Of course, the answer is yes! Christians are called to genuinely love everyone. But do you have to *like* them? Well, that depends, doesn't it? Are they likeable? Considerate, thoughtful, enjoyable to be around? Would you enjoy having them at your Thanksgiving dinner table? So we evaluate these folks largely the same way we would any other person who has newly come into our lives. We are free to like them if we find them likeable, but we are not required to like them. But we are required to love them.

However, they might be very rude and selfish. They might have personal values, attitudes, or behaviors that you can't accept. It is fine to say, "You know, I just don't care for that person very much" if you have good reason not to care. We should start out wanting to like everyone—even loving them as much as possible—until we are given strong and consistent enough reason not to.

"But this guy who is taking my son deeper into homosexuality is clearly not a nice man because of what he's doing," you might say. Yes, but it also makes your son not a very nice guy. You have to come to terms with the fact that that ship has sailed and make the necessary adjustments as so many parents must do on all kinds of issues.

But how does one do this in the proper balance of grace and truth? Well, it comes down to a very important and critical clarification. It requires us to make a distinction between the person and this particular relationship they are in. You cannot approve of the relationship if it is sexual. But this is about the person, your child's partner. You see, we all evaluate people—and whether we like them or not—based on who they are. And to a large degree, that is our call. We all get to pick our own friends and those we like and care for, don't we? And this situation is no different.

It is no moral compromise to decide that you indeed like your child's partner as a person. This has nothing to do with your convictions about the relationship itself, but about the person even though you have very strong disagreements.

3. But my son says I can't love him if I can't accept his partner.

This is a response that is sadly too common in these kinds of situations and no one should fall for it, frankly. We can love our children and not particularly like their friends or partners. The two are very different things. *This* is your child. *That* is your son's partner. Your love for the first is not contingent on your love for the other. And it is unfair—and actually manipulative—to put someone in the position of demanding that your love for them must include anyone else that is important to them. The world just doesn't work that way, and it doesn't and shouldn't here.

The proper and healthy answer to such a statement is simply, "Well, I'm sorry you feel that way."

But you must also ask, as in all situations, why you find yourself not caring for a particular person, whether or not you have really given this person a fair shake. What is it in you that might keep you from being able to like them? Is there something there that you need to come to terms with? Don't let the nature of their relationship keep you from seeing this person as God sees them and giving them a fair chance to be liked by you.

You must prayerfully search your own heart and let God expose things there that need exposing. No one is required to like everyone, but we are called to love everyone as much as we can and treat them as graciously and patiently as possible. If your child's partner is a human being, they deserve your general kindness, regardless of what you think of him or her.

4. *They want my blessing—what do I do?*

Now this question is quite different from the issues addressed in the previous few questions because it is not about people, but particular types of relationships. God is very clear in that we must love others, regardless of their stories. But this does not mean that we have to like or bless what they do.

> No one can be expected to give their blessing to something that goes contrary to their convictions.

Every relationship that we ever have has to navigate such parameters for a whole host of reasons. All of us have the experience of not liking or approving of everything our friends do. And we are free not to. And they are free not to approve of what we do. This is no test of our relationship. Love and approval are two very different things.

No one, loving parents included, can give—or be expected to give —their blessing to something that goes contrary to their beliefs and convictions. And they shouldn't be shamed or demeaned for not doing so, and certainly not by their son or daughter.

It is like your cohabiting son or daughter's relationship. You might like their partner very much but not approve of their living arrangement. Knowing how you feel about such relationships, it is actually inconsiderate for them to ask you to bless such a relationship. It is not you being unfair or judgmental. It is them—it is their issue. You simply answered the question you were asked. And your gay or lesbian child, as well as your cohabiting child, should be able to respect that and not push you on it. It puts you in a difficult place and good people don't do that to one another.

5. What about the sleepover?

Your child brings her lesbian partner home from San Diego for both of them to spend the Thanksgiving holiday with you. You have met her many times before as they've been together for nearly two years and she's very nice. You genuinely enjoy seeing her every time you have the chance. They will be staying four nights with you. This is an interesting situation that you never imagined you'd be in. How to arrange the accommodations?

Do you insist they stay in different rooms or allow them to sleep together, as they have been together for nearly two years? Sleeping together at your house is not going encourage them to sleep together more, as if they were teenagers or college students. It is not even likely to make them think that you know and approve of their sexuality and living situation, giving them a long-awaited green light from Mom and Dad. It's just staying over a few nights. So do you let them?

Bottom line: It's your house, your call. You should not feel forced to have something in your house you are not comfortable with, regardless of what it is. And the guest must follow your wishes. That is just basic manners. And the traffic goes the other way. When in their house, they make the rules. They don't want you smoking in their house. Guess what? It would be rude and more than thoughtless to demand you be able to light up.

And you shouldn't feel bad about this. I wouldn't bring a rack of ribs to a dinner party at my vegan sister's house. If she asked me to, or said it was perfectly all right, that would be one thing. But to just expect it would be okay because that's what I want, or thinking she needs to come to terms with the fact there are meat eaters out there and she'd better face it, is not being considerate of her. She wouldn't want such a thing in her kitchen, dripping on her cutting board, staining her knives, sizzling on her grill. If I can't understand why this would be a problem, that's my problem.

Your house, your rules. Their house, their rules. That's how it works. And it's basic politeness to respect that. No debate.

But if possible, it's important you talk about these things before the trip, again, just as if it was your son and his girlfriend. They need to know ahead of time that there will be separate sleeping arrangements, just in case they were expecting something different. It is likely that they could call you and give you a "heads-up" on what their plans are and expect you to be cool with it. No one gets to tell another what their own house rules are going to be, even if they tell you in advance. It doesn't matter. Nor does it matter if they are legally married. That is not a license to ask you to disregard your convictions.

And if they cannot abide by that, they can stay at a hotel nearby, or not come together. Such a request from the host is more reasonable than the demand from the guest that you ignore your own personal convictions in your own house.

What about a Wedding?

Regardless of whether you live in a state that has legalized same-sex weddings or not, the invitation to such a wedding is something that more are having to face. So how do you respond if you receive such an invitation from a family member—or for that matter, a close friend?

This is more difficult than it may seem—or at least there are more wrinkles and angles to it. I have thought about this a great deal and have discussed it with many strong Christians. Among those I greatly respect, there is curiously a good bit of differing opinion here and I can understand and respect most of these convictions. Some would give a flat-out no to any and all such invitations. While I understand and respect this conviction, I take a less absolute approach, even though my convictions about what marriage is and is not are *very* firm.

I will try to address this point with many of these different thoughts in mind. And this should indicate that, like many issues we address in these chapters, there is a not a clear yes/no answer. But there are helpful guidelines.

1. *Who's inviting you?* Is it the nice man in accounting at work who audits your team's budget? Or is it your brother or child? You will certainly evaluate these two invitations differently, one causing you much more soul-searching than the other. For me, the person would have to be very special and meaningful to me.

2. *What kind of wedding?* Is it happening in a Christian church or conducted by a clergyman representing the church? What kind of church? Is it an Episcopal or Lutheran church that permits such weddings, but should know better, or a Unitarian church that has forever been on the side of whatever challenges biblical convention? Two related questions that should weigh in your decision are (1) is it a completely secular wedding at the country club, the beach, someone's backyard, or even city hall, and (2) is it actually a legal marriage or a commitment ceremony?

3. *Do they know your convictions?* This is an important aspect to this decision-making process. The few friends whose ceremonies I might attend know quite well how I feel about such relationships and ceremonies. They would not think for a moment that my attendance means I'm softening on my convictions. They might even wonder why I'm attending. And if they asked me, it would give me an opportunity to explain precisely why I am there. I am not there to celebrate the relationship and the place it's moving to on

this day, but because I love them and I wanted to be here today for them. This is important for them to know, as it is honest about my regard for them.

Making the Decision

So what to do after you receive the wedding invitation? First, the wedding is not just about the couple, with everyone else mere spectators. The attendees are participants as well, supporting the couple, rejoicing with them in what their new union is creating, and even in standing in solidarity with them and their joining families, agreeing to be there for the couple, as a couple, in the years to come in many ways. You are a stakeholder in their union.

So when some Christians say they cannot in good conscience attend any kind of same-sex wedding, it is not necessarily because they don't like "those darned gays and lesbians" but because of what they understand a marriage and a wedding to be. Along these lines, I could not imagine myself going to a heterosexual couple's "commitment ceremony," declaring their dedication to each other, while not seeing marriage itself as necessary. Even if I cared deeply for the couple, I simply couldn't participate in celebrating such a thing. In fact, to be honest, I'd think it was silly.

> I would not want to be part of a seemingly Christian wedding that was clearly in contrast with Christian teachings.

And this would not be any kind of statement about the people themselves, as hard as that might be for some to believe. Would I think my atheist friend hated me if he declined my invitation to attend my baptism next week? Such an event is a massive thing to a believer, but it would be unfair for me to expect him to come, much less make it a litmus test for the substance of his appreciation for me. It is just a matter of belief and conviction about what such ceremonies are. Hopefully, such Christians could explain these convictions to their gay or lesbian family members or friends in a gracious way and hope to have the couple *understand* even though they will not likely *agree*.

This is where I would stand in most situations. I certainly could not attend a wedding that was held in a church or officiated by clergy as a Christian wedding that was clearly outside of God's design and desire for marriage. I would not want to be a part of a seemingly Christian wedding that was clearly in contrast with Christian teaching, for I would not only be an audience member but a witness and supporter, which, as was explained, is exactly what the friends, family, and loved ones at a wedding are. It is a communal covenant that all are entering into, but of course, two more than anyone else. This I could not do and would have to decline.

> What does it mean to be faithful to the church as we seek to love our gay and lesbian neighbors?

Are there other circumstances under which I would go?

It depends, and it would relate primarily to the first question: Who are these folks and what is my heart toward them?

My main consideration would rest upon what this person meant to me and how I wanted to communicate my love for them. Add to this whether the wedding was a secular affair or of a faith tradition outside Christianity that had no authority in my life.

For me, if I was ever to attend a same-sex wedding, these would be the questions that I would have to wade through. I will be honest. I do have some friends whose weddings I would like to attend, solely because of what they mean to me. These particular friends harbor no illusions about my convictions here. But I care for them so deeply as people— and as "opponents"—that I would be willing to reach out and attend their weddings just to show them that despite our clear differences, I would like to be there for them. And knowing each of them as I do, none of them would be married in a church, so that eliminates that issue. But it would be a very rare and selective event for me.

This might seem inconsistent on my part to some people, and I understand and respect them if they do not understand. But in more than a few issues regarding friendships with our LGBT neighbors, there are areas that are not as black-and-white as we might like them to be and on which good and faithful Christians will disagree. But that should not keep us from seeking to find the best way through them that are true and authentic to our faith, and gracious and loving to our friends.

So, for me, I would need to be very motivated to attend such a wedding, and I would do so primarily out of love for the person who invited me.

As you work through your own decisions in these matters, ask a number of Christians whose maturity and discernment you trust. Determine what is wise in their advice and apply it to your particular situation. Of course, give it a great deal of prayer. However, in terms of a hard line, I would say that a same-sex church wedding is something a Christian cannot participate in.

Questions—and Answers
for Our Churches

Central to every Christian should be the church, our Lord's beloved bride whom He is in the process of redeeming. So the question of loving our LGBT neighbors must include the most important institution we have in our lives. What does it mean to be faithful to the church as we seek to love our gay and lesbian neighbors? Are there irreconcilable conflicts here? Should we not welcome all?

What about churches that call themselves LGBT congregations? Is that what is needed to love our neighbors? Should there be such a split in the church? We will explore these important questions in this section. Let's start with the most basic.

1. *Do homosexuals belong in our churches?*

This is the first question we must ask, but it's not a hard one. We addressed it to some degree earlier. It can be easily answered with two straightforward questions: (1) Where else should they belong? (2) You're there with your sin. What makes you more deserving?

In Matthew 9, we read about a meal Jesus was attending and it caused the religious leaders some concern. If we are honest, it would have caused us some concern as well. Let's read:

> *And as Jesus reclined at table in the house, behold, many tax collectors and sinners came and were reclining with Jesus and his disciples. And when the Pharisees saw this, they said to his disciples, "Why does your teacher eat with tax collectors and sinners?" But when he heard it, he said, "Those who are well have no need of a physician, but those who are sick. Go and learn what this means, 'I desire mercy, and not sacrifice.' For I came not to call the righteous, but sinners." (vv. 10–13)*

Jesus told them—and us—that He belonged with the sinners and the sinners belonged with Him. Note that He reclined at their table. This means He made Himself comfortable there. That may make some of us readers uncomfortable.

We read stories like this and we know what the right answer is, right? Of course Jesus should have been with these people, we say. But if we are honest, would we have not been pretty much like the Pharisees? We are passing by Matthew's house one evening. Yes, Jesus is there because those are the folks who really need the Savior. But we look in the window. We are troubled, and not because Jesus is there but because he seems to be having just a bit too much fun with them. He's laughing at their jokes and seems a bit too comfortable with it all for our tastes. "He certainly doesn't look like he's 'saving' anyone. He just looks like one of the crowd," we conclude disapprovingly.

But neither did Jesus just hang with the sinners to make the scene. He was their friend because they needed a friend, especially Him. He told us it is the sick who need a physician. And a good physician, much less the Good Physician, will not allow his patients to remain ill. He does everything he can to make sure they are healed. If they don't want to be healed, he will do all in his power to convince them that health is better and is available.

> Do sinners belong in the church? Theirs are the only applications the church accepts.

And He told us He has come to call all of us sinners *to* something. To life, to holiness, to love, to acceptance, to repentance, to grace. He is both friend and Savior. He calls us on our stuff and helps us become new creatures.

Do sinners belong in the church? Theirs are the only applications the church accepts. All others go right in the wastebasket. As one pastor told me, "Sinners are the largest growth market there is in my line of work."

2. I have gays in my church. Should I avoid the "clobber verses"?

Some gays and lesbians call the verses quoted below "clobber verses." We all know them:

- You shall not lie with a male as with a woman; it is an abomination. (Leviticus 18:22)
- If a man lies with a male as with a woman, both of them have committed an abomination; they shall surely be put to death; their blood is upon them. (Leviticus 20:13)
- For their women exchanged natural relations for those that are contrary to nature; and the men likewise gave up natural relations with women and were consumed with passion

for one another, men committing shameless acts with men and receiving in themselves the due penalty for their error. (Romans 1:26–27)

- Now we know that the law is good, if one uses it lawfully, understanding this, that the law is not laid down for the just but for the lawless and disobedient, for the ungodly and sinners, for the unholy and profane, for those who strike their fathers and mothers, for murderers, the sexually immoral, men who practice homosexuality, enslavers, liars, perjurers, and whatever else is contrary to sound doctrine. (1 Timothy 1:8–10)

If you have gay and lesbian folk sitting in your pews, should you avoid these passages? This is not so much a question of LGBT folks in your church as it is one of how we preach and teach the Scriptures. Do the churches around Minneapolis's Mall of America have the Bible's materialism and coveting verses at the ready for visitors? Do churches in Las Vegas preach against gambling, prostitution, and bad Elvis impersonators every week? Do we look up the verses that will really make people squirm, or those that will really make people feel good about themselves? Good Bible-teaching churches teach the Scriptures in an engaging and clear way and let them speak for themselves.

> There are "clobber verses" on divorce, on gluttony, on lust, on gossip, on lying, on pride.

As a pastor in Bangor, Maine, memorably told me, "Listen, you can't be a preacher and not step on some toes. That's why I teach through Scriptures, book by book. That way, if someone has a beef with what the Scriptures say, they can read ahead and know when to play golf that morning."

Just be faithful to teach the Scriptures as passionately, truthfully, graciously, and clearly as you have been called to. Don't run *to* the hard stuff but don't run *from* it either. Just teach what comes next.

There are all kinds of "clobber verses" in the pages of Scripture—on lying, on lust, on pride, on divorce, on gluttony and gossip and greed. Yet there is no movement in the church today to re-interpret the scriptures to conclude that God is either neutral on or in favor of divorce, gluttony, lust, gossip, lying, or any other major sin. No one uses any of these as a prefix to Christianity. But this is precisely what is happening in so many quarters in the church today who try to convince us that "gay-Christian" is a legitimate thing. Prophetic pastors who want to be faithful to the age God has placed them in must realize that such unbiblical efforts require their clear denunciation and correction. But it's not the messenger who "clobbers" anyone. It's the message that does.

It is the faithful preacher who explains their clear meaning and intention when these verses come up. It is the unfaithful preacher who either chooses to avoid these texts or keeps coming back to them in inordinate frequency. Let the Word of God be the Word of God by teaching it in full.

None of us has the right to rewrite Scripture, but none of us have the right to pick out our own hobbyhorses from it either, whatever they might be.

An Open Letter to the Church

Below is a letter from a woman who is a Christian, a lesbian who lives with her longtime partner. She is fully aware of the gap between what her faith teaches and her current relationship. It is not something she ignores or tries to reconcile. She struggles with it. And while you might not agree with every point of her letter here, it is very much worth reading. It is instructive to those people and churches who try to reconcile same-sex sexual behavior and Scripture and give all a pass on their own sin.

To the church concerning homosexuals and lesbians:

Many of you believe that we do not exist within your walls, your schools, your neighborhoods. You believe that we are few and easily recognized. I tell you we are your teachers, doctors, accountants, high school athletes. We are all colors, shapes, sizes. We are single, married, mothers, fathers. We are your sons, your daughters, your nieces, your nephews, your grand-children. We are in your Sunday School classes, pews, choirs, and pulpits. Many choose not to see us out of ignorance or because it might upset your congregation. We ARE your con-gregation. We enter your doors weekly seeking guidance and some glimmer of hope that we can change. Like you, we have invited Jesus into our hearts. Like you, we want to be all that Christ wants us to be. Like you, we pray daily for guidance. Like you, we often fail.

When the word "homosexual" is mentioned in the church, we hold our breaths and sit in fear. Most often this word is fol-lowed with condemnation, laughter, hatred, or jokes. Rarely do we hear any words of hope. Many of us recognize our sin. Does the church as a whole see theirs? Do you see the sin of pride, that you believe you are better than or more acceptable to Jesus than we are? Have you been Christlike in your relationships with us? Would you meet us at the well, or restaurant, for a cup of water, or coffee? Would you touch us even if we showed signs of leprosy, or AIDS? Would you call us down from our trees, as Christ did Zacchaeus, and invite yourself to our house as our guest? Would you allow us to sit at your table and break bread? Can you love us unconditionally and support us as Christ works in our lives, as He works in yours, to help us all to overcome our own sins?

And to those of you who would change the church and its

teaching to accept the gay community and its lifestyle: you give us no hope at all. To those of us who know God's Word and will not dilute it to fit our desires, we ask you to read in John's Revelation, the letter to the church in Pergamum:

> I have a few things against you: You have people there who hold to the teaching of Balaam, who taught Balak to entice the Israelites to sin by eating food sacrificed to idols and by committing sexual immorality. Likewise, you also have those who hold to the teaching of the Nicolaitians. Repent therefore! (Revelation 2:14–16)

You are willing to compromise the Word of God to be politically correct. We are not deceived. If we accept your willingness to compromise, then we must also compromise. We must therefore accept your lying, your adultery, your lust, your idolatry, your addictions, YOUR sins. "He who has an ear, let him hear what the Spirit says to the churches."

We do not ask for your acceptance of our sins any more than we accept yours. We simply ask for the same support, love, guidance, and most of all hope that is given to the rest of your congregation who need redemption. We are your brothers and sisters in Christ. We are not what we shall be, but thank God, we are not what we were. Let us work together in obedience to God's Word to see that we all arrive safely home.

A Sister in Christ[1]

---

1. Used with permission from the anonymous author and Hunter Baker, at whose website this open letter is posted. See "An Astonishing Message from a Gay Sister in Christ," *Great Southern Prose and Ideas Company* blog, March 18, 2013, http://hunterbaker. wordpress.com/2013/03/18/an-astonishing-message-from-a-gay-sister-in-christ/.

3. *What about homosexuals in the church who don't seem to want to change their ways?*

Now this question gets us into the meat of things. Most would agree that gay and lesbian folks in our community should come to our churches, for how else might they meet our Lord?

But what if they don't seem to be getting to know Him quick enough? Or . . . if they seem to be getting to know Him fine, but not changing quickly enough, what do we do?

These are important questions, because they get to the heart of what matters: our relationship with Christ, our ongoing journey in Christian discipleship, and our redemption. Ask any pastor, Sunday school teacher, or small group leader. They will tell you this is a messy process. No one really seems to be making the progress that we think they should. *We* don't seem to be making the progress we think we should. So do we give up and not expect anything from any of us? Of course not.

The first thing anyone learns of Jesus is that He called people, called them to leave what they were doing—mending nets, collecting taxes, burying their loved ones—and follow Him. Stop doing that and come do this! Both He and His cousin John called *everyone* to something very specific and definitive:

In those days John the Baptist came preaching in the wilderness of Judea, "Repent, for the kingdom of heaven is at hand." (Matthew 3:2)

From that time Jesus began to preach, saying, "Repent, for the kingdom of heaven is at hand." (Matthew 4:17)

John appeared, baptizing in the wilderness and proclaiming a baptism of repentance for the forgiveness of sins. . . . Jesus came into Galilee, proclaiming the gospel of God, and saying, "The time is fulfilled, and the kingdom of God is at hand; repent and believe in the gospel." (Mark 1:4, 14–15)

So [Jesus' disciples] went out and proclaimed that people should repent. (Mark 6:12)
"No, I tell you; but unless you repent, you will all likewise perish." (Luke 13:3)

This is the message He has for all who would seek to follow Him. No one is immune or excused from its demand. Now here is the frustrating part, making church work messy. Sometimes full repentance is immediate, like suddenly being healed of sickness or addiction. Often it is a process. I had to repent of my sin when I first came to Christ at the age of seventeen. Some things were taken out of my life immediately; some, not so much. I am still repenting of my sin, even some of the same sins. This is what Christian discipleship is for all of us, and it cannot be avoided.

But what about folks who've been coming to our church for months or longer but don't seem to be interested in repentance, in having a renewed mind, and turning from their sin?

This can be a tricky one and not just in the area of one's sexuality. How do we determine what progress should be made at what point in our walk with Christ? Should progress be evident? Of course, for there must be signs of the fruit of God's Holy Spirit taking hold within us, and an increasing death to the flesh within us and the growth of the fruits of His Spirit. Jesus tells each of us that we are to abide in Him as the true vine, and from this we will bear fruit in keeping with repentance. But this happens differently for all of us, and to judge others by our own process is not how God does it.

But as our question above asks, what about people who seem to have no interest in repentance? A friend told me about an older man, very quirky and unique, in a home group he taught for years. He loved to come and never missed a week. But he was a salty fellow, clearly unredeemed and quite happy to tell you as much. They would ask him, "Rob, are you interested in ever becoming a Christian?" He would answer with something like, "Haven't seen a need to in all my days. Don't reckon I'll see one tomorrow." His group would shrug its shoulders. But when asked why he kept coming, Rob would answer, "'Cuz I like you people, and I reckon I'll keep coming as long as you'll have me." Rob was never disruptive or constantly challenging what was being taught. He was just part of the group, so of course they told him he was welcome.

Maybe God would finally move in Rob's heart one week and do a great work there. Maybe He never would. But as long as Rob wasn't disruptive or otherwise ill-tempered, who were they to disqualify him from that wonderful possibility? Jesus tells us in John 16:8 that it is the Holy Spirit who convicts us of our sin. And He does it in His own timing. We serve Him.

However, we are not to leave that job completely up the Holy Spirit. We are not oafish bystanders with our hands stuffed in our pockets but His helpers in loving people, teaching the Word, challenging one another to fidelity and good works in Christ. But only the Spirit can bring real repentance and change. He can do it without us, but we can't do it without Him.

> Sin disqualifies us from teaching God's Word. Temptations do not.

So we have to trust people to the Holy Spirit, just like my friend did with Rob.

4. *What if they want to become members, get baptized, receive communion, teach Sunday school?*

These are very important questions as well. Regardless of who you are or what your story is, church membership, baptism, communion, teaching within the church, serving as a lector are not rights. They are responsibilities that require some serious commitment of behavior and belief.

When one becomes a member of a church, he is becoming a

member *to* and *of* something. That something has requirements and expectations. Among many are to be faithful in word and deed to the teaching of the church and to Scripture. One must be seeking to be an obedient disciple of Christ, and submitting oneself to the redeeming and demanding grace of Jesus. Where issues of faith are at stake, Rob could not have become a worker in the church because he hadn't bought into what Christianity was about. What if he wanted to make sure the church van kept running, clean the classrooms, stack the chairs, help organize the church picnic? His help would be most welcome because it was not an issue of fidelity to faith. But what about teaching a Bible class? Even if Rob had been the professor of ancient Middle Eastern cultures at the local university, he would not be eligible because he did not ascribe to the essential tenets of the faith.

Often in the Scriptures, the words "baptism" and "repentance" are used together, as each requires the other.[2] Entry into the church requires a real, observable commitment and dedication to something very specific, as does membership into nearly any community. We can welcome into the church those who seem uninterested in, or taking a long time to show, any sign of conviction of sin or sense of repentance. Such people should not be excluded from our midst, but neither should they be made leaders or full participants in the life of the body, regardless of their story. There are clear qualifications for those who are being baptized, receiving the body and blood of Christ, or entrusted with teaching God's Word—even if it's with crayons, scissors, and glue to kindergarteners.

And, as we have seen, it is important on questions like this to remember that having sexual desire for people of the same sex is not a sin in itself, just as my having a desire for someone who isn't my spouse is not a sin. *But it's what we do with that desire that makes it sin and very seriously so!* It is a sin to lust on a sexual attraction. And it is a sin to act on

2. Matthew 3:2, 8, 11; Mark 1:4; Luke 3:3, 8; Acts 2:38; 19:4.

a sexual attraction outside of God's boundaries between that of a husband and wife. It is not a sin to be tempted by it.

So, there is nothing about being same-sex-attracted that disqualifies one from such duties and privileges in the church. It is being obedient to the call of Christ in the midst of such desires that matters, and this is a requirement of all. Those who willfully live in sin without repentance should be disqualified for a season from such responsibilities in the church until a significant time of forgiveness is sought and healing and correction has been received.

Sin disqualifies us from teaching God's Word. Temptations do not.

5. What about congregants who won't approve?

This one is easy. There are two types of folks here and each must be treated differently. There are:

1. Good-hearted folks who are simply challenged by others' stories they just don't understand. It is for many of these folks that we have developed this book. They just need to have it explained to them who Christ came to call: sinners. Ask them who the sinners are that Christ came to call. And who is excluded from that category of people called "sinners"? Is there anyone who shouldn't be included? These Christian sisters and brothers are unsure of the right thing to do. They must be gently and directly instructed.

2. The others are those who are not so good-hearted, but they think they are. They are "righteous"! They think they know who the good people are and they know who the bad people are. And they know where each belongs. These people are prideful, like the Pharisees. They need a good shake and strong rebuke.

Jesus was gracious and instructive with those of His day in the first group. And today is still "His day" and He remains gracious and instructive. So must we. Of the second group, He reserved His harshest words and judgment for them. And He does so for such folks today.

6. What about those who are disagreeable and disruptive?

From time to time any pastor and his church leadership will encounter individuals in their congregations who are part of their body—perhaps members, maybe not—who just like to create waves. You wonder if they truly believe it's their spiritual gift. What about folks who are coming to your church somewhat regularly and have moved beyond asking honest questions about biblical faith and practice and seem to be set on challenging both biblical and ecclesial authority? This is an important question. Like so many others in these pages, it is important to see it not as an LGBT issue but a body of Christ issue, for this is exactly what it is. (It is also a basic issue of decent manners.)

Many years ago, in a church where I was in leadership, we had a husband and wife who led worship for us and after some time they started doing so barefoot. The first time, we noticed it, but didn't ask about it. Just thought it was a "thing" for them that week. The next week, they did it again, and our pastor asked them about it: "Uh, so what's with the shoes?" They explained that God told them to do that because when they worship they are on "holy ground" and, therefore, should take off their shoes to show respect. It was actually just weird.

It wasn't a big deal in one sense, but it was in another. First, they just started doing it on their own when they should have discussed it with and explained their new "calling" to the leadership of the church. Just run it by someone. We are all under obedience and accountability to God, but also to the leadership that He has established in our particular church body. These two go together 99.9 percent of the time. They refused to get in line with what the leadership of the church thought best and were asked to step down from their leadership role. They had gotten obnoxious about holding on to their new no-shoes revelation, and our pastor encouraged them to remain faithful to it, but just to do so from their pews from now on.

No body of believers—as well as any group of people who are trying to participate in a shared mission—can tolerate attitudes and practices of disagreeableness and dissension among their members and attendees. And it is not difficult to tell the difference between those seeking answers to honest questions that they don't understand and those just wanting to kick up dust. The first deserves patience. The second deserves no patience at all and strong leadership to nip it.

Such people should be privately confronted about their behavior and have it explained why it's not healthy, individually and for the larger body. They are not the only folks to be considered in such a situation, but those in the congregation who have to increasingly live in the midst of such division and disruption. Your church leadership should act quickly to make sure this kind of constant questioning and challenge is taken "off-line" immediately so that it is not a public spectacle. Explain to the individual or group why such behavior is problematic and not in the spirit of Christ.

If it persists, have the same conversation with them, but this time with a few other leaders from your church, and perhaps a friend they might have who is a more integral part of the congregation. Explain again the problem with such behavior and attitude and let them know the next step will be being asked to leave the congregation and that you really hope it doesn't have to come to that. Firmness in love and love in firmness. This is true of all disagreeable people in your body, regardless of what their story might be.

7. Some churches have created official statements on sexuality. Should ours have one?

Developing a congregational or denominational statement on human sexuality and practice is a very smart idea and can be very helpful to the congregation as a whole. It not only serves as an objective and clearly articulated statement of belief that is needed in times of correction, but also as a teaching resource for the larger congregation, explaining that this is what we believe the Scriptures teach about human sexuality, who we are as male and female, and why it matters.

And it is much easier and cleaner to develop such a statement in advance than when your church is in the thick of such a controversy and the statement is being drafted "on the fly" to bring the disagreement to a resolution.

There are several things to consider when drafting such a statement.

1. Make sure it is, in its greater substance, a positive statement about what it is the Bible teaches about sexuality as a gift of God. It should certainly address the prohibitions but mainly do so by contrasting it with the careful and biblical teaching of what sex is for, why it is what it is, and in how it is to be practiced solely between a husband and a wife. This is what Jesus did in Matthew 19 and Mark 10. He gave His listeners God's original ideal for marriage and sexuality, and then all else is evaluated in light of those statements.

2. It should be done by consulting a larger group outside of your congregation. Consult theology professors at your denominational seminaries or Bible schools, other respected pastors in your city, perhaps leading Christian experts on sexuality. Wisdom comes from a multitude of counselors.

3. Similar to point #1, do not make it personal or specific to addressing a particular problem. Make sure it teaches and proclaims a fully biblical teaching on God's view of and desire for human sexuality. This should be a statement of what the Bible teaches about sexuality and what your church believes and practices, rather than a whip to bring

certain people in line. It should speak to and be helpful to the whole body of Christ.

4. But do make sure it clearly addresses the issues that are and might likely come up in your congregation(s) so that everyone is clear on what this entails. Of course, it must speak to much more than just the same-sex issue. It should address questions like the understanding of the nature and importance of male and female, what the sexual relationship is for, and who it may and may not involve. It should also address the issues of cohabitation, divorce, and forgiveness of sexual sin, as well as issues of fertility, which will be increasingly relevant in your community. What are the boundaries regarding artificial reproductive technology (for single and marrieds), surrogacy, natural adoption, and so on?

8. *How much respect should homosexuals expect?*

By now, given what we have learned, you should be able to answer this question easily: *They should expect just as much respect as you would show anyone else who came to your church.*

And likewise, you should expect the same sense of responsibility of these new attendees as you would from anyone else. They are no more or no less special and valuable than anyone else who will ever walk through your doors.

9. *What about LGBT churches?*

This is a good and important question.

First, there are many kinds of churches that are founded and function to serve certain groups of people. There are cowboy churches—big where I live. There are biker churches. There are Korean and Chinese churches here in the States, and I have attended Western, expat churches in China. The first church I ever went to as a teenager was a surfer church. It was not strange for us to wear our baggies, surf shirts, and flip-flops to church when the break was particularly good on a Sunday morning. The older folks there figured, "Well, at least they come to church!" rather than skipping and going straight to "Point-Break Fellowship," as we called it when we would occasionally skip the Sunday service.

People go to such churches not so much because they want to do church "their way" but because they want to be a church and do church for those who are similar. We can have our views on whether the body of Christ should be organized as such in different demographic groups, but it doesn't come from an impure motive. And like my surf church, it was a welcoming passageway for me and my mates into the body of Christ.

So what about LGBT churches? The largest such particular body is the Metropolitan Community Church, founded solely to minister to the LGBT community. Are they another community-specific congregation like Cowboy Church?

It might seem like it, but there is an important angle that cannot be ignored. While it is good for the leadership of these congregations to seek to minister to folks in the LGBT community, it is not good, as with any congregation, to reinterpret the Word of God to accommodate that congregation. It is well-known they take a very different, unorthodox view of Christian sexual ethics. It is a key hallmark of theirs. This is putting one's desires, interests, and understanding of themselves over the clear, consistent, and historic teaching of God's Word. No good Christian is permitted to do this. Nor is it really helpful to those they are seeking to minister to, as explained in the open letter to the church we read on pages 155–57.

And it must be noted that heterosexual believers have been fudging on the faith since the early days of the church. Most of the New Testament consists of apostolic letters to correct such abuses in orthodox Christian teaching. Most of the synods of the first few hundred years of Christianity were held to clarify and proclaim sound doctrine in the face of heresy and wrong doctrine. So rewriting the Scriptures to fit one's view of the world is not confined to any one community or age. But it cannot be tolerated and must always be resisted by Christ's people.

This reminds me of a very clear and concise statement that H. Richard Niebuhr, the famed Yale Divinity School professor, made about a particular kind of "we-won't-ever-tell-you-you're-wrong" theology of his day. He said it created a make-believe reality where "A God without wrath brought men without sin into a kingdom without judgment through the ministrations of a Christ without a cross."[3]

No congregation or minister does anyone any good by intentionally lowering the cost of discipleship for those it is charged with serving and building into disciples of Christ.

10. *Can we reasonably coexist?*

Of course we can, and we must. But it is a mistake and misunderstanding to assume that coexistence means full agreement or total acceptance of ideas, beliefs, and practices. Nor does it mean ignoring our differences as if they don't exist. As we have tried to illustrate through these pages, we are called and commanded to treat ourselves and all we come in contact with, with both grace and truth.

Grace tells us there is always hope, love, forgiveness, and redemption for all, regardless of what we have done or who we are.

Truth tells us that there is something larger and more demanding of us than our own desires, beliefs, and natures.

We are all convicted and condemned by the second. We are all pursued and pardoned by the first. *All of us.* Love recognizes both of these, always in equal measure.

---

3. H. Richard Niebuhr, *The Kingdom of God in America* (Harper & Row, 1937/59), 193.

7

NAVIGATING THE DILEMMAS WE FACE IN OUR SOCIETY

Of course issues of gender and sexuality have been part of the mainstream of many cultural debates over the last four to five decades. They have become political issues ever since the Supreme Court established a constitutional right to birth control for both married and unmarried individuals, abortion through the whole nine months of pregnancy, and the larger social issues of sex education in schools, dealing with sexually transmitted diseases in public health care, coed dormitories, cohabitation, adultery, and fornication laws.

Sexuality is often seen as a very personal issue, and it is, but it also has very public consequences as all of these issues and more remind us. In fact, anthropologists tell us that marriage arose in all cultures at all times for many social purposes, chief among them being the regulation and social control of sexuality, because unchecked, it can have consequences that are especially damaging to women, children, and the larger society.

So, the LGBT issue is about more than our friendships with

individuals and what one does in his or her own bedroom. It has very public ramifications. We must consider how to deal with these issues in relation to our desire and effort to make meaningful friendships.

Four Fundamental Questions

Clearly Christians should care about and influence opinion and decisions made in the area of gender and sexuality. Here are several questions on these topics to consider in our local community and the nation.

1. *Should I support or oppose gay rights?*

This is a slippery question, as it makes a no answer seem wrong and unfeeling and a yes response considerate and noble. But as Christians, the answer is that we must oppose them as stated and for reasons that *affirm* our LGBT neighbors. Confused? Let me explain.

All Christians should strongly support human rights. In fact, before Christianity, the idea of universal human rights was largely nonexistent. Christianity had much to say and do in changing this globally.

Each and every same-sex-attracted person is fully human, which is an obvious statement, but must be said. Therefore same-sex-attracted people should and do have the right to full human rights.

But when we start to divide people and give them particular rights based on something unique about them, we actually serve to diminish their humanity. Their particularity becomes their distinguishing mark, rather than it being their humanness. The LGBT community holds that their sexual orientation is just like one's race or ethnicity, and this is a major point in their political efforts. As we saw in chapter 3, there is no scientific or empirical support for such a claim. But do you find groups of people working for Asian, Latin, African, or Salvadorian rights? What they each have a right to, and we all must advocate for where these are denied, are *human* rights.

During the civil rights movement, black men wore signs during demonstrations—particularly at the Memphis sanitation workers strike, which was the reason Martin Luther King Jr. came to the city where he was killed. Those signs declared a very important and simple truth: I AM A MAN. The British and American abolitionists used the question in their pamphleteering: "Am I not a man and a brother?" when making the case for the full human rights of those being bought and sold as slaves. Those oppressed by the Dred Scott decision asked in response, "Am I not a man?"

These were dramatically important and necessary social statements. And they were not qualified. I am human, therefore I should have the rights anyone else has. They did not demand their rights because of or based around some measure of uniqueness but for their commonality with everyone else. Their humanness.

So, should we support human rights? Absolutely, without reserve or apology. But gay rights? To base one's rights on something particular to them is contrary to the idea of human rights. Is that not the definition of exceptionalism?

2. What about same-sex marriage and civil unions?

This is an important question as well, for many reasons. One, it occupies so much bandwidth in the public discussion. Two, while marriage may seem like a private matter between the couple, it is a very public issue. That is why all cultures at all times have some set of publicly recognized, enforced, celebrated, and encouraged mores and rules that anyone from any other culture would recognize as marriage. Likewise, it has always been, until the last few milliseconds of human history, a relationship exclusively between men and women. And this is not just true in conservative, Christian, religious, or developed cultures but all cultures. It has been a universal and pan-historical human value, even if it allows for multiple spouses.

So same-sex marriage, as some cultures have begun to define it today, is contrary to historic and universal human practice. It is also contrary to the Christian understanding of marriage, clearly explained in

Genesis 1 and 2, and in Christ's crystal-clear affirmation of this design in Matthew 19 and Mark 10. So Christians cannot support same-sex marriage because it is contrary to what marriage is according to our faith and how God created humanity in its sex-distinct duality. And marriage is a big deal in the Christian story. Check out Ephesians 5:31–32 and Revelation 19:7–9. We don't have the option to support something that is contrary to what God created and established.

But neither should we support it as a civil matter, because it is an inherently experimental family form, driven solely by adult desires and wishes, and no society has ever raised a generation of children in same-sex homes. All virtuous societies care for children being raised in motherless or fatherless families. No caring society intentionally creates them for children for the sole reason that some adults desire such families. Whenever a culture seeks to create new family forms, replacing the married mother and father norm, they have never shown the form to be a wholly successful means to obtain and promote adult, child, and societal well-being. The social science of the past fifty years in the midst of all manner of family formation change has been quite clear and conclusive on this. Every child has a fundamental human right to be raised and loved by its biological or adoptive mother and father. The same-sex family says they don't because of the kinds of families the adults in that family desire. So, among many things, this is a compassion isssue centered on the needs of children.[1]

---

1. Glenn T. Stanton, *Why Marriage Matters: Reasons to Believe in Marriage in a Post-modern Society* (Colorado Springs: Piñon Press, 1997); Glenn T. Stanton, *The Ring Makes All the Difference: The Consequences of Cohabitation and the Rich Benefits of Marriage* (Chicago: Moody, 2011); Glenn T. Stanton and Bill Maier, *Marriage on Trial: The Case against Same-Sex Marriage and Parenting* (Downers Grove, IL: InterVarsity Press, 2004); Kristin Anderson Moore et al., "Marriage from a Child's Perspective: How Does Family Structure Affect Children, and What Can We Do about It?" *Child Trends Research Brief* June (2002); Mary Parke, "Are Married Parents Really Better for Children?" *Center for Law and Social Policy Brief*, May (2003): Sara McLanahan and Gary Sandefur, *Growing Up with a Single Parent: What Hurts, What Helps* (Cambridge: Harvard University Press, 1994); Judith Wallerstein, *The*

What about civil unions, then? Many might see these as a good compromise. "I can't support redefining marriage for various reasons, so civil unions seem like a good way to give same-sex couples something of what they are seeking," the thinking goes. However, it is necessary we understand that no mainstream leader in the LGBT movement supports civil unions as an answer, believing they solve any issues of equality or justice. Just the opposite—they see civil unions as "less than." They contend such a stance makes the social statement that gay and lesbian people are not deserving of *this* (marriage) like everyone else, but we can just give them this next best thing (civil unions).

The Human Rights Campaign, one of the largest and most effective LGBT advocacy groups in the world, judges civil unions in these strong words: "Make no mistake, civil unions single out a group of people for second-class citizenship. That is discrimination and it doesn't belong in any [law]."[2]

Supposing that one is supporting the LGBT community in advocating for civil unions or domestic partner benefits is an illusion. It's actually seen as insulting by nearly all LGBT leaders, and therefore your support is seen as insulting.

Good friends make sure they understand what their friends on another side of an issue are actually wanting or not before they make decisions on what they assume are helpful compromises. It is similar to

---

The Unexpected Legacy of Divorce: A 25 Year Landmark Study (New York: Hyperion, 2000); Linda J. Waite and Maggie Gallagher, *The Case for Marriage: Why Married People Are Happier, Healthier, and Better Off Financially* (New York: Doubleday, 2000); Claire M. Kamp-Dush and Paul R. Amato, "Consequences of Relationship Status and Quality for Subjective Well-Being," *Journal of Social and Personal Relationships* 22 (2005): 607–27; James Q. Wilson, *The Marriage Problem: How Our Culture Has Weakened Families* (New York: HarperCollins, 2002); W. Bradford Wilcox et al., *Why Marriage Matters, Second Edition: Twenty Six Conclusions from the Social Sciences* (New York: Institute for American Values, 2005).

2. "HRC Deeply Disappointed in Kerry's Support of Massachusetts Constitutional Amendment," Human Rights Campaign Press Release, February 26, 2004.

advocates of same-sex marriage seeking to protect religious freedom by assuring us that pastors will not be required to perform same-sex wedding ceremonies, as if that is the only threat to religious freedom there is on this issue. It shows they are not really thinking about addressing or understanding their opponents' concerns. It ends up being insulting rather than helpful. We must be mindful of the same types of things.

3. What about this issue in the workplace?

First, regardless of the issue, it is never good to politicize the workplace. You are there to do a job, to make the donuts, produce the widgets, satisfy the customers, make money for the shareholders, and then go home. This is true for all issues, even the ones you believe in. So, in terms of coworkers educating, persuading, inviting, and challenging you to get on their political bandwagon at work, it is usually not a good idea.

If you have same-sex-attracted people working with and for you, and it is likely that you do if you work for a large company, it is good to befriend those you can connect with. You don't have to try to be their best friends or even weekly lunch buddies. But it is important, at least, to reach out and let them know you are interested in them as a person and are willing to establish a friendship if they are interested. This is a sign and action of grace. Think about how you might be able to help them in their tasks or in navigating the professional processes or social circles at your work. If they do a particularly good job at what they do, take the trouble to tell their supervisor as you would (and should) for anyone. If you are known as a Christian at your workplace, this can have a profound effect on your personal witness as well as a strong message to other Christians at work who might not think it "kosher" to befriend gay, lesbian, or transgendered ("*those!*") people.

As in all situations, be yourself and be your friendly self. As you develop such genuine friendships, be willing to introduce them to other friends of yours at work, showing that you are happy for your relationship and you want others to have the same benefit. But the pursuit of such relationships should be natural and comfortable like any other relationship.

If such an individual is talked about unkindly behind their back, you should be the first to speak up in their defense, even if they have not become your friend. This is truly loving your neighbor and being a leader for what's right in your workplace. These same things can and should be true of LGBT neighbors as well.

4. *Shouldn't our religious beliefs be kept separate from our community values?*

Many Christians feel that their private faith belongs only in their church pew or at home, having no place out in the public square. Anything else is being a busybody or a do-gooder, and who likes that?

But read through the Gospels and the book of Acts and see what Jesus and the early Christians did. Their faith was dramatically public. They were very much "busybodies." Consider the Christians who built and ran foundling hospitals for abandoned babies, hospitals for the sick, soup kitchens for the hungry, job training for the un- and under-employed. Think about the abolitionists and leaders of the civil rights movement. They were deeply motivated by their faith in their important work.

Think about the Christians who are usually the first to show up with all types of aid to the victims of natural disasters like those of Hurricane Katrina, tornado-ravaged communities in the Midwest, and devastating wildfires in the western states. These are largely and even nearly exclusively Christian citizens and neighbors. They are certainly inserting their faith into public life. In fact, a nation's public life would be much weaker if people of faith were not involved, even in issues of morality. In fact, all of the above are issues of morality, are they not?

We can and should even be involved in issues of sexual morality and the family. The test of our virtue and kindness is not whether or not we are involved in such issues but in what manner we engage them and our opponents. For the friends I have on the "other side" of this issue, we are often both working very hard against one another and we know it. During certain state initiatives, we will often be invited to train and organize local citizens, speak at their rallies, do media interviews, and write articles and talking points in favor of their effort. We all take this work, and our commitment to it, very seriously. And yet we remain friends.

Much of this is because we try to do our work honestly and fairly. When I do an interview or write an article for some initiative, I think, "What if one of my friends from the other side read or heard this. Would they think it was fair?" This helps to keep me honest. I don't want them to think, "Man, that is a nasty shot that Glenn took!" or "Sheesh, he knows that's not true!" So I try to write and speak with care. I am pretty sure they do the same, because we will pick up the phone or draft an email to call each other on such things from time to time and sometimes we don't come to a resolution. But we do get to speak our piece and hear theirs. These friendships keep us all the more honest when we step onto the public square with our deeply held convictions. And that's good.

Does Sexual Freedom Trump Religious Freedom?

To bake the cake, or not to bake the cake? That is the question . . . at least regarding what kind of cake it is and what it's for. It's the same for taking pictures at or providing flowers for same-sex ceremonies. What do we do with service providers who refuse to do same-sex ceremonies due to conflicts with their faith or conscience?

The stories are well-known: bakeries that refuse to do wedding cakes, wedding photographers who explain that they cannot take the couple's wedding pictures, private owners of B&Bs who do not allow unmarried heterosexual or homosexual couples to stay in their house, churches refusing to rent out their activity halls for same-sex receptions, faith-based adoption agencies who will not place children in same-sex homes. These and more have all faced serious legal challenges, requiring them to face long, expensive legal fights and fines because of their convictions.

For both sides, it seems a clear-cut question. In fact, Chai Feldblum, a Georgetown Law School professor and an appointee to the federal Equal Employment Opportunity Commission (EEOC) by President Obama, believes the topic is quite cut-and-dried. She famously told one newsweekly that when religious and sexual liberties clash: "Sexual liberty should win in most cases. There can be a conflict between religious liberty and sexual liberty, but in almost all cases the sexual liberty should win because that's the only way that the dignity of gay people can be affirmed in any realistic manner."

Beyond ignoring the dignity of people of faith, what are these few instances where religious liberty should win out? Feldblum is clear: "I'm having a hard time coming up with any case in which religious liberty should win."[3] So much for "coexisting."

Many Christians, and a notable number of same-sex advocates,[4] believe that religious conviction and general dissent should not be eclipsed by the claim of sexual freedom. How should Christians feel about and approach such things? How do we thoughtfully balance individual rights and freedom of conscience? Is such refusal hateful and bigoted? The first thing to address is the rhetoric behind this issue.

Disagreement Is Not Discrimination

It is the basic assumption among far too many that the only reason one would choose to not provide such service is because of their hateful homophobia and bigotry. For too many, this is an obvious and

---

3. Maggie Gallagher, "Banned in Boston: The Coming Conflict between Same-sex Marriage and Religious Liberty," *The Weekly Standard*, May 15, 2006; For her fuller case, see Chai Feldblum, "Moral Conflict and Liberty: Gay Rights and Religion," *Georgetown Law Faculty Publications* January (2010): 119–21.

4. Just three examples are "Freedom to Marry, Freedom to Dissent: Why We Must Have Both," A Public Statement, *Real Clear Politics*, April 22, 2014; William Saletan, "The Photographer's Story," *Slate*, March 7, 2014; Conor Friedersdorf, "Refusing to Photograph a Gay Wedding Isn't Hateful," *The Atlantic*, March 5, 2014.

unquestionable script. But the accusation is often made without any actual proof, or even contrary to proof, similar to the experience of the anthropology PhD student in chapter 3. The provocative writer Dan Savage regularly makes this blanket assumption, describing such people as "hater bakers" (his words) and claims they should just be honest and put signs in their bakery windows letting everyone know, "We Don't Serve Gay People."[5]

Mark Joseph Stern, who covers gay issues at *Slate*, writing about the well-known story of the New Mexico photographer who resisted shooting a commitment ceremony, says those trying to defend her because she refused this job in a gracious and civil way are "dressing up her homophobia in good manners . . . " and then parrots Savage's ugly judgment: "But the ultimate effect of her actions is the same as if she had placed a sign on her shop door stating 'No Gay Couples Served Here.'"[6]

In fact, Stern is so sold on the truth of this assumptive narrative that he featured as evidence a newspaper article that told the story of a same-sex couple who were refused service in a Franton, Kansas, restaurant that astonishingly posted a sign that said, "No Gay Eating Here." The couple looked at the sign with legitimate disbelief while a customer told them, "It means you and your boyfriend can't come eating in here no more unless you find God." Another hollered, "You need God and the Bible." Stern didn't question the veracity of the article because he is sure such things happen regularly out in the "God, guns, and glory" heartland. In his zeal, Stern failed to appreciate that there is no Franton, Kansas, and the story was made up by a website whose stock in trade is drafting ridiculous spoofs.[7] It was a made-up story and ridiculously so.

---

5. Dan Savage, "A Baker Refused to Make Your Wedding Cake?" *SLOG*, Feb. 27, 2014.
6. Mark Joseph Stern, "A Polite Homophobe Is Still a Homophobe," *Slate*, March 6, 2014.
7. Mark Joseph Stern, "Ross Douthat's Canny (and Utterly Dishonest) Defense of Homophobia," *Slate*, March 3, 2014. The spoof story was: Haywood Bynum III, "Kansas Restaurant Kicks Gay Man Out, Tells Him 'No Gay Eating Here,'" *Topeka's News* (no date). After pulling his link to the made-up article, Stern looked high and

Now, while some who refuse to provide their services for alternative couples might be motivated by hate or bigotry, it is simply unreasonable, irresponsible, and uncivil for anyone to simply assume such. It is plain wrong to accuse someone of such beliefs without any real evidence or personal experience. There's a word for such assumptive judgments: "prejudice." Conor Friedersdorf from *The Atlantic* makes this very case:

> In America, there is plenty of homophobia, plenty of antigay bigotry, and plenty of people whose antagonism to gays and lesbians is rooted in hatred. Sometimes the language of religious liberty is used to justify behavior that is anything but Christ-like. But [mere assumptions of such beliefs are] implicitly trafficking in its own sort of prejudice. The working assumption is that homophobia, antigay bigotry, and hatred are obviously what are motivating anyone who declines to provide a service for a gay wedding.
>
> That assumption is wrongheaded.[8]

Is It Just Because the People Are Homosexual?

Many in this debate like to make it very personal, that it's the people themselves who are being refused and not because of the event or the particular request. They are refused for who they are rather than the event itself, as evidenced in the "No Gays Served Here" accusation from

---

low, finally locating a replacement article from a small community paper to support his case. This new story involved a janitor at a Walmart in Chickasha, Oklahoma, who told a same-sex couple they would have to leave the store because they were homosexual. Walmart investigated the story and said they "vehemently denounce the actions of this janitor" and were "appalled" at the incident. The janitor was fired. Clearly, such behavior is not policy nor tolerated in the least by the massive retailer. The incident was the action of one intolerant man.

8. Conor Friedersdorf, "Refusing to Photograph a Gay Wedding Isn't Hateful," *The Atlantic*, March 5, 2014.

folks like Savage and Stern. It is an important distinction and positioning it this way is rhetorically very effective because it makes it about the individual and their mistreatment. Few would not be outraged if a business were to actually hold a "no gays served here" policy. And they should be. If this were what it was about, it would be a persuasive and honest case. But it's not actually. There are clearly other issues behind such refusals, having nothing to do with the individual.

Let me give you an example very close to home. At Focus on the Family, we have our Whit's End children's area in our visitor center, which is a very popular play area and tourist attraction in our city. We have specially decorated rooms where families can come and have their children's birthday parties free of charge. They don't have to be supporters of Focus or even Christians. Muslims have come. They just have to have kids who are excited about celebrating their special day. And we are thrilled to help them do that. We don't ask people their story first to make sure we approve of them. We don't ask whether the parents are actually married. We don't ask their political preferences. We don't ask their religious identity. We don't ask their sexual preferences.

In fact, if a same-sex couple came and desired to have their child's birthday party there, we would graciously welcome them as we would anyone else and be as excited for that child's big day as we would for any other child. Indeed, one same-sex couple did ask if they could have their boy's birthday party there. We said, "Of course" and were happy to do so. Does this mean we are going soft on our conviction about homosexuality? Not at all, no more than it would mean we were going soft on our conviction of God's existence and goodness if we hosted the birthday party of a child with atheist parents. We are always happy to help celebrate a child's birthday—any child. We can get way behind that, and we do.

But what if for some reason this same same-sex family wanted to celebrate their family adoption party at our campus? That would be a different matter, given our strong conviction that all children have a fundamental right to be raised by a mother and father, of which a same-sex family by definition fundamentally excludes. We could not and would not facilitate such an event and shouldn't be forced to do so or accused of ugliness because of it. They would be asking us to participate in the celebration of something we cannot celebrate. And, of course, it would not mean we couldn't celebrate the child as a child. We just couldn't celebrate the intentional formation of the family itself. But we can and will always celebrate the birthday of any child. Anyone should be able to honestly understand the difference between the two.

Another example: A church in Canada refused to rent out their church hall for a reception for a lesbian wedding. They were brought before a human rights commission. Did they "hate" lesbians? They would have refused their hall for a commitment ceremony for a cohabiting heterosexual couple and a polyamorous or polygamous group. They would likely have also refused the use of their hall to the local evolution, nudist, or Hell's Angels club. They would refuse their space to Islamic, Mormon, New Age, and Hindu groups that wanted to have a party there. If the logic follows, that church must hate polys, evolutionists, nudists, bikers, and those of other faiths, as well as members of every other group they might ever refuse use of their facilities. But it is only some same-sex couples who contend they were rejected for *who* they were. Additionally, don't all of these other people have basic rights of assembly? Of course they do but they don't have the right to make anyone or any group facilitate their assembly. Reasonable people make allowances for such things as conflicting beliefs, and this issue should be no exception.

People in all professions refuse the business of others due to personal conviction, and it doesn't raise issues or make the people feel personally rejected. I have a baker friend who says he refuses plenty of jobs because of his moral convictions and never gets accused of injustice. Recently he said "thanks, but no thanks" to a job making a cake for a fraternity party in the shape of the body part where a thong goes, thong included. He regularly refuses actual requests for cakes shaped into sexual body parts. The photographer in New Mexico says she consistently refuses requests from pregnant moms who want nude pictures of their pregnant selves. She just doesn't feel comfortable doing them, and she doesn't. This street also runs both ways. Some same-sex proponents warn their peers against drawing firm lines like Feldblum's, explaining that this would also infringe on their right to refuse providing professional services they personally oppose. What about a gay photographer's right to refuse a family's request to shoot their daughter's confirmation ceremony being held at a church that takes a strong stand against homosexuality? Should he be allowed to say no? Should the parents respect his right to not violate his convictions or do something that would clearly make him uncomfortable? Of course.

Would they take his refusal as a personal judgment against them? They shouldn't.

Does this mean he hates Christians? He might, and only he knows for sure. But it's wrong, disrespectful, and illogical to assume that.

And let's be honest, would it be wrong of that family to initiate legal action against the photographer for his decision? Indeed, a drastic and uncalled-for overreaction.

So, serious question: Why do we separate and elevate the refusal to do a same-sex couple's ceremony, but never question the refusal of so many other groups or individuals when they do so? When I ask this question in a public talk at a university, I am always answered like clockwork with, "Well, no one can refuse service to someone because of race or ethnicity!" and the campus crowd erupts in thunderous applause. But there's a problem with such a seemingly obvious and persuasive response.

But You Can't Refuse
Service to African Americans or Laotians

Plain and simple, race and ethnicity and sexual orientation are two very different things, not alike. Race and ethnicity is a function of our heritage and genetics. We are what our parents, grandparents, great-grandparents, and our great-great grandparents are. It tells us who our "people" are. And it is not true of some of our natural siblings and not others. It is fundamentally objective, right down to the blood that flows through our veins. It truly is *who* we are.

However, as we saw in chapter 3, there is simply no objective or scientific evidence that same-sex or bisexual attraction or transgender identity is either wholly or even primarily genetic, passed to us through our family line.[9] They are not the same thing and when people proclaim they are, they are either ill-informed or simply being dishonest. It is not reason or objectivity that drives this but mere unsubstantiated ideology. And wishing or firmly believing something to be true—as radical atheists often tell us Christians—doesn't make it true. So there is no requirement that a compassionate, tolerant, and gracious person buy the analogy.

Regarding the nature of one's sexual orientation and its origins, the APA holds, "Sexual orientation is commonly discussed as if it were solely a characteristic of an individual, like biological sex, gender identity, or age. This perspective is incomplete because sexual orientation is defined in terms of relationships with others . . . Therefore, sexual orientation is not merely a personal characteristic within an individual. Rather, one's sexual orientation defines the group of people in which one is likely to find the satisfying and fulfilling romantic relationships that are an essential component of personal identity for many people."[10]

Further, the APA states directly, "There is no consensus among scientists about the exact reasons that an individual develops a heterosexual, bisexual, gay, or lesbian orientation. Although much research has examined the possible genetic, hormonal, developmental, social, and cultural influences on sexual orientation, no findings have emerged

---

9. *Answers to Your Questions: For a Better Understanding of Sexual Orientation &*
Homosexuality, an informational pamphlet published by the American Psychological Association, 2008.
10. *Answers to Your Questions*, 2008, 1.

that permit scientists to conclude that sexual orientation is determined by any particular factor or factors. Many think that nature and nurture both play complex roles…"[11]

Note their use of the word "develops" and not the definitive or objective "is." People do not develop a race or an ethnicity. It is what they are. No science comes close to making the same assertion about one's sexual orientation.

But, as some might contend, same-sex-attracted people are a minority who face cultural discrimination at many turns and therefore should receive special protection and attention. But is this entirely true anymore?

If someone would incorrectly state publicly on television, radio, the Web, or a newspaper that same-sex-attracted folks are ignorant, delusional, and the cause of nearly all of history's ills, there would be huge blowback. And there should be—for such statements have no basis in fact and stem from pure ignorance or rhetorical thuggery. But say the same about religiously serious people, particularly Christians, and you're a smash on the nightly Bill Maher show or the Richard Dawkins lecture circuit. Sheer maturity and civility require one to denounce both types of comments.

But in popular culture today, it is obvious even to a hermit that making fun of the one group is excused as entertainment and roundly applauded. But what happens when a sports figure, musician, actor, or journalist comes out of the closet? There is no backwoods backlash from the unenlightened bumpkins. Rather they are widely and joyously lauded for their bravery. But what is there to be brave about when nearly every cultural elite and mainstream news outlet enthusiastically sings your praises? The victim script is increasingly challenged every time we are reminded how many citizens are moving in support of gay causes. If

11. *Answers to Your Questions*, 2008, 2.

the increase of one means anything, the shrinking of the other has to be the result.

We must recognize that a wedding is a sacred and serious thing for most people. It is a celebration and affirmation of something very specific. Stopping by your shop and purchasing a nice box of red velvet whoopie pies or getting a family portrait is another thing altogether. People of faith should be able to refuse participating in the first via their services, but not necessarily the second. Folks who refuse to participate in or provide their services for weddings and such are not refusing to serve individuals as individuals but for what they are being asked to be a part of. But if the same-sex couple wants to come get some pies from you for their Fourth of July celebration or birthday party, they should be welcomed as any other customer. Again, the difference here is not hard to appreciate.

This is the heart of the issue: people of religious conviction cannot and should not be allowed to generally discriminate against anyone, but neither should they be forced to participate in or support with their services ceremonies and events that directly violate their religious or moral convictions. No one should.

Bathrooms: Boys, Girls, Other?

Just as cakes, flowers, and photos have become flash points in our culture, so have bathrooms. Bathrooms for transgendered people, that is.

A student or a worker decides they should live as the opposite of their gender, and they make the necessary early changes in dress and physical presentation, then perhaps undergo hormonal treatments and surgery. This requires many life adjustments for the individual, to be sure, but one that is getting a good bit of news and stirring up passionate discussion is which bathroom do they now use and which locker room do they change in? This debate is even taking place among parents and school officials concerning elementary-age children.

This is really much ado about nothing in terms of actually working out the bathroom deal. LGBT activists on many campuses lobby strongly for what they call "gender-neutral" bathrooms and you can find them marked this way on college campuses. Given my interest in such things, I often take note of them, and they are typically bathrooms to be used by one person at a time. In other places—hospitals, restaurants, malls—they are marked as "bathrooms." Single-use bathrooms. Other times they are designated with both the male and female symbol, letting the user know it's open to all.

They work the same way, regardless of what they are called. If the door is locked, you wait your turn. If it is not locked and no one is in there, it's all yours, regardless of what your gender story is. No biggie. So why would LGBT groups on so many campuses advocate for distinguishing these facilities as "gender-neutral" when it's obvious that they are? It's a good question, and to be honest, I believe it has to do primarily with gender politics. It is an opportunity for the campus to be recognized as trans-friendly, regardless of whether it makes any actual difference in solving any practical problems for a trans person.

But what about times when the need arises and there are only sex-distinct restrooms? For many trans people, it's not really a big deal. They often use the restroom that coincides with the gender they are presenting themselves as. If people see the person as a woman, the individual uses the women's bathroom and will use a private stall to do their business. Like most people in a restroom, they tend to be discreet. Seldom is it a problem. Few people question a bathroom mate on whether they are truly a man or a woman, even if they have doubts. Just do your business, wash your hands, and move on.

What about at work, where people are more likely to know your story and there are no single-user facilities? If the person is known to be trans, then it simply becomes a function of working it out with the human resources department at the workplace and finding a solution that works for everyone, if indeed one can be found. It is unlikely any business could install a restroom facility for just this one employee, primarily out of sheer practicality. And it can have nothing to do with a lack of sensitivity toward the trans person. Usually the structure of the office space simply cannot accommodate it relative to space and the plumbing it requires. They just have to find something that works for all, like other problems that arise when people have to share spaces together.

When the subject arises at middle and high schools, most schools provide their students use of a single-use facility, usually found in the teachers' lounge. Most times, this works wonderfully. But in some rare instances, the parents are set on making an issue out of the problem and will usually explain that it is embarrassing and troubling for their child to be the only student to have to go use the teachers' restroom. This concern is hard to take seriously. Going to use the teachers' facility is more traumatic than going to use the girls' restroom when all your classmates know you to be a boy? Seriously?

This solution shows a very reasonable, good-faith effort on the part of the school administration to accommodate the child's felt need. The child is far less likely to be teased—if at all—for going to the teachers' lounge than going among either his or her own classmates. And the other children must be considered as it is not close-mindedness or insensitivity that makes them uncomfortable in having to use the facility with a child they know to be of the other sex. Their feelings matter too.

> You can "love people" and never really interact with any.

Frankly, this issue is usually an issue of sexual politics rather than mere practicality. But all people should do what they can to find a solution for everyone involved that makes everyone as comfortable as possible in these instances. That goes for the comfort and assurance of the trans person as well as the men and women who also have to use the restrooms.

A reasonable solution can always be found that protects the dignity of all if everyone seeks to act reasonably and give up any particular agenda they might have, no matter where they might be coming from on this issue.

Display Love and Follow Your Convictions

Dealing with issues like these can be confusing, intimidating, and uncomfortable because they are relatively new to our culture and therefore foreign turf for so many of us—like driving through the streets of Shanghai. But remember that your LGBT friends are out of their comfort zones as well. For many of them, those nutty Bible-believing Christians can be intimidating. To them, we are "those people." And one of the fun things about being "those people" regardless of what kind of group "those people" are is busting the stereotypes about "those people."

It really comes down to remembering and being faithful to two things. The first one is the most important.

First, *love the person*. This is different than loving people. "Loving people" is conceptual and impersonal. Loving the person is different. Consider God and you. Which statement would you be most attracted to, "God loves people" or "God loves Susan"? It's the person who matters. You can "love people" and never really interact with any. But loving Susan requires that you spend time with and get to know Susan.

Be very intentional, natural, and genuine in loving the person in front of you. Make it about them. And think about making sure they feel and experience that love. If you do this and the other person knows it from his or her experience with you, you can mess up in many ways relationally, but your commitment and care for that person will, to paraphrase the Scriptures, "cover a multitude of relational mistakes." That love will be the thing that helps you work through them, not *if*, but *when* they happen.

Second, *be true to your convictions*. There is no genuine friendship that hinges on whether or not you see the world—or the important issues in the world—the same way. If it does, that's a conditional friendship and therefore no friendship at all.

Friends try to understand the other's beliefs, views, and convictions like you might try to understand what and why a socialist believes what they do. And you want to respect them inasmuch as these beliefs are important to your friend. Of course, you don't have to respect the idea, but friends do respect that their friend takes it very seriously. You might argue about, discuss, and tell your friend they are wrong, but we respect them and do so for the cohesion of our friendship.

But the same is true of them toward you. Don't be ashamed of, hide from, or make excuses for what you believe. You might make a stand for it in the wrong way, be thoughtless or unfeeling, and that must be addressed and learned from. But it is not wrong to believe that your convictions and beliefs should be respected. In fact, to do so as a two-way street is a sign and indication of honoring the other. It's part of what a friendship is.

Sure, neo-Nazis and Jews may not be able to coexist as friends or a Klan member and an African-American. In fact, no reasonable person should be able to coexist with a Klansman or one who sees the value of genocide now and then, but most other folks with disagreements and differing views of the world can create and maintain meaningful relationships. And for one to say that Bible-believing Christians and gay or lesbian people being friends is precisely analogous to, say, a neo-Nazi and a Jew and or a Klansman and an African-American, as we have seen many do, is just simply beyond the pale. As well, some Christians say we should not develop friendships with gays and lesbians because "light doesn't mix with darkness," as I was once told. Both views are unsupportable and wrong.

Love the person and be true to who you are and your convictions. And allow the same of your friend. These two truths will guide you through many thickets.

CONCLUSION

WHY ALL THIS MATTERS

So here we are at the end of the book. Hopefully it's the beginning of your pursuit of many important and rewarding new relationships, for you and your potential friends. Learning the importance of and ways to make friends with our neighbors who identify as gay, lesbian, or transgendered challenges us, broadens our understanding of others as well as ourselves, and simply makes life more interesting. As Chick-fil-A president Dan Cathy said in chapter 4, it's "the blessing of growth." This is true of all kinds of relationships.

Each of the questions and topics we've addressed in these chapters is critically important, not because of the questions themselves but because of what's at the heart of them. They are all about forging and growing real relationships. And think about this: relationships are the most important and meaningful things going on in the universe. That's not hyperbole. They lead to everything else that's good in the world. In fact, Christians must understand that relationship is the first and most divine thing in the world.

Before the Beginning of the World

Consider what existed before the beginning of the world. It was, of course God, but a very unique God: One God in three persons—Father, Son, and Holy Spirit—who from eternity past exist in beautiful and loving union with one another and they each ever rejoice in this. It is really their essence and substance as divine persons. That means relationship—love, giving and receiving, closeness, enjoyment of others by just being together—is a fundamental quality of God and therefore, humanity, which alone is created in His image. It is certainly a divine thing, even when it's just sitting at a coffee shop, catching up with someone and simply enjoying their company. That is what our Father, Son, and Holy Spirit do, have done from eternity, and will continue to do eternally: glory in and be astoundingly content in each other's company.

> We cannot sell out our friends, but neither can we sell out our faith.

Their relationship is an end in itself, good for its own sake; and therefore so must ours be. Whenever we relate to, connect with, and befriend another, it is a very holy thing as well, whether we realize it or not. Literally. In it, we are doing what God does and being what God is.

Therefore, thinking about, asking questions, and getting answers on how to develop and maintain relationships with others is profoundly important, and especially for the Christian because of what and who our God is and what He made us to be as His children in the world. This splendid truth alone will serve as a true and wonderful guide in developing and maintaining such relationships.

As we close, let's consider and be mindful of some basic qualities and attitudes we must keep in the front of our minds and in our hearts as we seek out these relationships.

Be Faithful

A friend is faithful to a friend. They hang in there through hard times, hurt feelings, and misunderstandings. But we must also walk the necessary balance between that commitment and our commitment to our faith and convictions. We cannot sell out a friend, but neither can we sell out our faith. This is one of the struggles that make certain relationships—not just with our gay and lesbian friends but with all kinds of people—both difficult but also worth the effort. The object is to find the place where you can be faithful to both, relationally "walk and chew gum" at the same time.

Be Loving

Christianity is a hard calling because we are not only called to love others but to go further and love those who hate us. And if we are called to love those who hate us, we are certainly called to love those who disagree with us. And love is not conditional; you do this for me and I'll do this for you. Remember the story of Esperanza in chapter 4? She continued to love and serve her son's partner even while he was tremendously hateful and abusive to her. She was in for the long, rocky, unconditional haul. Such commitment is not super Christianity but mere Christianity.

Be Truthful

Friends shoot straight with each other when it's called for. Now this doesn't mean we do it all the time, for those who do don't keep friends very long. But we must live in truth and fidelity to our convictions *and* to our friend. At the same time, we must respect and accept this in our friends. Now this doesn't mean we don't try to persuade our friends to our way of thinking. We do this in all relationships and we learn how to do it graciously while not damaging the friendship.

Someone important said, "Treat others as you would want to be treated." We must also be willing to be challenged by our friends and change parts of our understanding, behavior, and attitudes when it is called for. Nobody gets all things right all the time, so adjustments are always needed, and this shows humility.

Be Wise

Know up from down, truth from fiction. As we explored in chapter 3, there are too many taking one or the other side of false extremes on these issues and not being aware of or ignoring the critical nuances between them, therefore working from a false foundation. Do the tough work of finding out the nuances, the importance of them and the truths found therein. Also, know what limits are essential in such relationships and how to graciously maneuver through them. Much of the equilibrium of living in grace and truth in all our friendships requires a humble wisdom.

Be Informed

Wisdom is different than knowledge, as those with plenty of knowledge are not always wise. But wisdom requires a good and judicious handling of knowledge. Know what you should know, stay informed on issues, and grasp what the story is on them. We've discussed two examples from both sides of this issue in previous chapters. Many well-meaning Christians believe civil unions are a reasonable compromise on the marriage issue, but no mainstream leader in the LGBT community believes they are. They actually find them discriminatory and therefore offensive. Not helpful. And many non-Christians believe that conservative Christians take the entire Bible literally. There is not one believer who does or ever has. Most take the Bible seriously, truthfully, authoritatively, but recognize the difference between literal, poetic, and figurative portions of Scripture. Holding to stereotypes and assumptions about what others believe doesn't help or honor anyone. It tells the other person you are not even interested in knowing who they are and what they believe.

Read widely on various issues you want to learn about and read from the most reasonable leaders and proponents of that position. There you will learn what mainstream belief in that community is and why they hold to it. Be informed.

Be Strong

Developing such relationships is not easy. There will be rough spots, as there are in most relationships. But the nature of the differences here makes it especially difficult. Both of you will have to deal with voices from your own communities who ask—and it is more of a statement than a real question—"What in the world are you doing being friends with *that* person?" It gives you an opportunity to explain why such relationships are important and about why "*this*" person is special enough to deserve your friendship. This is another conviction you will be called to stand by.

Be Influential

This last point is very important. We need more people on both sides of this issue being influential, demonstrating to either side that real and civil relationships can be had in spite of the real differences between us. When John Corvino and I decided to start doing debates together around the country as often as we could, we agreed that one major value in doing so would be to demonstrate to students and faculty that these issues can be engaged in very spirited and passionate ways but also civilly. We agree that if that is all we accomplished, that was worth the effort because a vibrant democracy demands that we engage those we disagree with, doing so thoughtfully with substance and respect as people and fellow countrymen. Sadly, such examples are in short supply.

At the beginning of our events, people took our friendship with a grain of suspicion, but afterward often commented, "I didn't think two people with such polar opposite views on this issue could be real friends, but you guys really seem to be. And it doesn't prevent you from challenging each other." That is the kind of influence we hoped and tried to have, showing folks on the far right, the far left, and everywhere in between that significant disagreement and honest, valued friendship are not oil and water. Living in this way is extremely countercultural, out of the box, and therefore influential in society today. People want to believe that it is possible to live—and flourish—this way. You can help them.

Jump in. There's plenty of room in the pool for a few more folks like you and your new friends.

AFTERWORD

We end this book by coming back to where we started, but hopefully with more insight and wisdom. It is important that the church and each of us who make up Christ's body—regardless of our role and responsibility—be *prophetic*.

This word is very important and is often confused with things like predicting the future or perhaps growing a long beard and yelling when you have something spiritual to say. (Women prophets can just yell louder and more sharply to make up for the lack of facial hair.) Being prophetic is something much more than this. Jesus talks about it in Matthew 16:1–3:

> And the Pharisees and Sadducees came, and to test him they asked him to show them a sign from heaven. He answered them, "When it is evening, you say, 'It will be fair weather, for the sky is red.' And in the morning, 'It will be stormy today, for the sky is red and threatening.' You know how to interpret the appearance of the sky, but you cannot interpret the signs of the times."

It has to do with what we discussed in the introduction concerning David and the sons of Issachar, their capability of discerning the times in which God placed them and ability to live faithfully in them, calling the church to be what it needed to be for that time.

Each believer lives in a particular generation with its own blessings, opportunities, challenges, and dangers; and thus, we are called to be faithful, discerning, and life-giving in the unique generation in which we are placed. To be able to do so requires that we be prophetic. It means that we learn to have eyes, ears, and hands that can see, hear, and touch the spirit of the age in which we live, knowing how to apply and live out God's grace, truth, and life among our time. It means that we understand the present time, are able to take a full measure of it in light of God's Word and His Spirit, and see what it uniquely requires of us.

It also means that we have the voice to speak, the hands to work, and the feet to carry us in doing what needs to be said and done. This is being prophetic, and it's what God calls each unique generation to.

Think about so many of the great names of our faith throughout the history of the church. Peter and Paul knew what their unique calling was in the early days of the establishment of Christ's church in the world. The early fathers, Athanasius and Irenaeus, were the great theological lions who revealed and stood against the destructive heresies threatening the life and purity of the church. Consider the great Augustine, whose strength of spirit, wisdom, and example helped navigate the church through the tumultuous times of the decline of the classical world and its transition into the Middle Ages. Catherine of Siena, who much later worked tirelessly and faithfully to bring peace between the warring factions of church and state. The teenaged Joan of Arc, who led the fight and died to help free her mother country of France from the domination of England in the Hundred Years' War.

In more recent times, consider Dietrich Bonhoeffer, who knew that the Nazi genocide must be opposed and gave up his quiet and safe academic life to join the resistance. The Reverend Martin Luther King Jr. knew his people needed strong, principled, and nonviolent leadership in the effort of throwing off their oppression and abuse. Pope John Paul II helped to launch Solidarity, the Polish citizens movement, which ultimately led to overthrowing the communist domination of Poland and helped pave the way for the end of the Cold War. Dr. John C. Willke and Francis Schaeffer early on realized what the sin of abortion was doing to women, to the unborn, and to a civil society, and spoke out tirelessly and forcefully against it. Each understood the times in which God had placed them and fulfilled His purpose for them.

The same is true for us today. We have many challenges we are called to engage in obedience and fidelity to God and His will for us. Some of them are *against* certain things, others are *for* things. And we need to know which is which, even, as we have seen in these pages, within particular issues themselves.

The mainstreaming of homosexuality in society and the redefinition of marriage and the family that render them genderless institutions have never arisen in any age of the church before like they are today, because these are historically and culturally unique and novel developments. And so, never have Christians had the call and opportunity to interact with, enter relationships with, and befriend those who are involved in and working for these social and ideological changes. There is no past generation for us to observe how *they* did it. We are it. We're the ones on the stage, with camera rolling. We are the generation that following ones will look to see and learn from. What will our example be? What will they be able to learn from us and will it be an example worth following and emulating? Or will we teach them to do just the opposite because we got it wrong or merely shrunk from the challenge?

We are answering these questions now, whether we like it or not and whether we realize it or not. Much of that answer depends on whether we get one critical balance right: dealing with the issue itself in *truth* and the people it involves in *grace*. Of our precious Savior, it was said,

And the Word became flesh and dwelt among us, and we have seen his glory, glory as of the only Son from the Father, *full of grace and truth*.[1]

---

1. John 1:14, italics added.

As Christians, we are to incarnate Jesus in our communities through our words, our actions, and our relationships in a world that desperately needs to experience Him through real, honest day-to-day connection with those who are inhabited by Him.

Glenn does conferences for churches and groups, providing encouragement, advice, and educational stories and examples on the topics covered in these pages. These range from one-evening events to weekend retreats. Details are available at glenntstanton.com.

More from Glenn T. Stanton

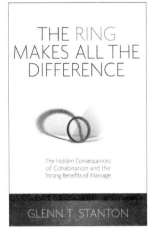

THE RING
MAKES ALL THE
DIFFERENCE

The Hidden Consequences
of Cohabitation and the
Strong Benefits of Marriage

GLENN T. STANTON

978-0-8024-0216-5

Drawing from an absolute well-spring of the most respected mainstream research, Glenn T. Stanton explains how all relationship forms are not equal. Cohabitation is not living up to its promises and widely held assumptions. It actually decreases one's chances of marital happiness and achieving lasting love. It is associated with significant declines in every important measure of happiness, health and well-being while marriage increases them by large measure. And according to the best research, living together tends to harm women more than it does men. In this book, Glenn shows us why relationships are not equal. Truly, *The Ring Makes All the Difference.*

"Christians believe traditional marriage matters because it is outlined for us in the pages of sacred Scripture. But guess what? Science, reason, and history are also on our side. In this excellent book, my friend Glenn Stanton explains how all of these roads point to the importance of marriage" –Jim Daly, president, Focus on the Family

Also available as an ebook

MOODY
PUBLISHERS

FOCUS ON THE FAMILY®

Welcome to the Family

Whether you purchased this book, borrowed it, or received it as a gift, thanks for reading it! This is just one of many insightful, biblically based resources that Focus on the Family produces for people in all stages of life.

Focus is a global Christian ministry dedicated to helping families thrive as they celebrate and cultivate God's design for marriage and experience the adventure of parenthood. Our outreach exists to support individuals and families in the joys and challenges they face, and to equip and empower them to be the best they can be.

Through our many media outlets, we offer help and hope, promote moral values and share the life-changing message of Jesus Christ with people around the world.

Focus on the Family MAGAZINES

These faith-building, character-developing publications address the interests, issues, concerns, and challenges faced by every member of your family from preschool through the senior years.

For More INFORMATION

🖥 **ONLINE:**
Log on to
FocusOnTheFamily.com
In Canada, log on to
FocusOnTheFamily.ca

☎ **PHONE:**
Call toll-free:
**800-A-FAMILY
(232-6459)**
In Canada, call toll-free:
800-661-9800

THRIVING FAMILY®	**FOCUS ON**	**FOCUS ON**	**FOCUS ON**
Marriage & Parenting	**THE FAMILY**	**THE FAMILY**	**THE FAMILY**
	CLUBHOUSE JR.®	**CLUBHOUSE®**	**CITIZEN®**
	Ages 4 to 8	Ages 8 to 12	U.S. news issues

Rev. 3/11